The P

B44/08

The Priestlike Task

A Model for Developing and Training
the Church's Ministry

Wesley Carr

First published in Great Britain 1985
SPCK
Holy Trinity Church
Marylebone Road
London NW1 4DU

British Library Cataloguing in Publication Data

Carr, Wesley
    The priestlike task.
    1. Church of England – Clergy
    I. Title
    262'.143   BX5175
    ISBN 0-281-04146-6

Filmset by
Dorchester Typesetting Group Ltd
Dorchester, Dorset
Printed in Great Britain by
Ebenezer Baylis and Son Ltd
The Trinity Press, Worcester and London

The moving waters at their priestlike task
Of pure ablution round earth's human shores.

J. Keats

Contents

Preface

Behind this book lie nine years of reflection upon and work at the question of ministry in the Church of England. Progressively I have come to believe that there are two fundamental stances, which are mutually informative, upon which genuine development of the Church's ministry can take place. One is theology, the distinctive discipline of the Church; the other is a dynamic understanding of human institutions, among which the Church is numbered. The present essay is chiefly about the application of these insights to contemporary issues of organization and training. The book which explores the theoretical connections between these two disciplines has yet to be completed

Much of the original research was done under the auspices of Chelmsford Cathedral Centre for Research and Training. This was the realized vision of the late Dick Herrick, with whom I worked for a while, and for whom this little book is a small act of *pietas*. A distinguished series of consultants advised the Centre on its progress – Dr Kenneth Rice, Dr Pierre Turquet, and most recently, Dr Eric Miller. The approach to interpreting institutions which they created and consolidated at the Tavistock Institute of Human Relations is that adopted here. The Reverend Bruce Reed of the Grubb Institute has written a pioneering attempt to use this approach to interpret process and movement in churches. My book tries to build upon this by exploring some of the practical consequences for organization and training of viewing the Church in this way. My debt to each of those mentioned is incalculable. All have contributed much, knowingly and unknowingly; the errors that remain are attributable only to me.

In any writing today the question of gender presents acute discomfort. Since there is no simple term for both male and female in English, I use male forms with generic reference. Except where for obvious, and regrettable, reasons this cannot yet apply, 'clergy' is used for all authorized ministers.

Behind any such writing, especially when extensive use is made of experience, lie the contributions of colleagues. Many churchpeople, particularly in the Diocese of Chelmsford, have helped, as too have associates in the work of the Tavistock Institute and the A. K. Rice Institute (Washington-Baltimore Center), with whom I have had modest connection. Two friends outside both of these worlds read early drafts and were critically encouraging. To the Reverend Canon Peter Pavey and the Reverend Albert Radcliffe I offer my thanks. Mrs Susan Hewitson deciphered my voice on tape and my handwriting on paper with persistent patience.

Footnotes have been kept to a minimum. Any direct quotation has been annotated. Some of the more general ideas which underlie sections of the argument may be followed up in other books. A few of the key texts are listed under the heading of 'Further Reading'. But the real test of the argument and the conclusions drawn from it is whether it resonates with the experiences of the reader. In matters of ministry these are as, if not more, important than any theoretical text.

Chelmsford Cathedral   WESLEY CARR
August 1983

Introduction

This is an essay in applied theology. From an examination of how people behave in and towards the church an interpretation of its task, and therefore of its ministry, is proposed. To exercise this ministry some organization and training are required, and most of the book is about these two issues. The defined context of the argument is the ministry of the church – the Church of England – set in a particular environment. Such specificity may in these ecumenical days appear to be perverse. But treating ministry in this way enables us to avoid a number of pitfalls. There can be no shift to what ought to be or towards positing aims for this church without first examining carefully what it is already about. This is the reason for the persistent reference to the church's task – that which it actually performs. Churches are human institutions, made up from human beings who live and work with other human beings. Speculation, fantasy and the way in which such a body is held in the minds of those to whom it offers ministry are more significant than is always realized. In a general theological investigation of Church and ministry such fundamental matters are difficult to discover and assess. But by taking a specific church these facets of institutional life become prominent and unavoidable for the student. In facing such perceptions and examining them lies hope of genuine and profitable change.

The argument of this book, however, should not be of interest to members of this one church alone. The ecumenical dimension in reflection on these questions may expose the prejudice and narrowness of some positions and at the same time the breadth of unacknowledged agreement. The risk, however, is that being institutionally non-specific any such overview can allow each separate church to take for itself what it already approves and to dispose upon others

1

those things which it does not like. But it is these very things that compose much of its own life and beliefs, whether they are acknowledged as such or not. By dealing with one particular church, therefore, we may be able to enable such covert questions to be exposed. They can then be looked at in the context of each separate church's life and ministry.

The word 'priest' and its cognates appear frequently throughout the book. How they are used and how they may be recovered will be explored. But here two preliminary comments may help readers orient their minds to the subject. 'Priest', 'priesthood' and even 'priestlike' are all controversial terms. A definition of how the term is used in the present work will be found in the chapter on the model of ministry (Chapter 2). Some contemporary problems and questions associated with the concept are examined in Chapters 3 to 6. Priesthood is, however, invariably used to describe a model and not to endorse any particular position with regard to today's debates on the theology of priesthood, least of all one that becomes preoccupied with individual priests. Only by escaping from so narrow a perspective may the church's priesthood be recovered. The other word to note is 'development'. There is a ferment in the churches around questions of Church and ministry. A number of exciting ideas are being generated. This book is written as a contribution to the search for proper and necessary change. But one aspect of applied theology is that it has to take account of things as they are. Hence the notion of development, which implies moving from what is to what may be, and doing this as much by recognizing resources within the present structures and systems, which have not been fully utilized, as by finding new ones.

1

Thinking about the Church and its Task

The word 'church' arouses a variety of responses. Some instinctively think of buildings, although even that view is complex. What is a delight to an architect may be a financial liability to a treasurer, an obstacle to mission for a pastoral committee, and a loved centre of worshipping life for a congregation. Others may think of denominations. To others the church is the body of Christ, a congregation of believing people, which becomes visible when it gathers for worship or some similar activity. Any attempt, therefore, to interpret the Church when thinking about organization and ministry requires a framework by which these and many other standpoints can be taken into account. Only then can all the available evidence be assessed in such a way that it can be sifted and examined without any being presumed to be irrelevant or inappropriate.

Much thinking about the Church and ministry is concerned with aims and aspirations. Christians often reckon that they already know what ought to be done. This is then set down and people are invited to aim at some new standard of church organization or life. Exhortation has its place. But if we are to determine some framework or model upon which organization and training for ministry can be built, we first need to examine the evidence of what is the case. But even here the variety of approaches demands some sort of discernment. For example, statistics of membership, attendance and finance are all important as means for establishing a profile of a local church. But these cannot give due attention to other less tangible factors, such as the impact that the church is making on those who are not members, the range of personal ministry which is offered by priest and people, and the value of the local church as a focal point for the parishioners. Yet most clergy value these things most highly among all that might be said of a church. It is not surprising that they can bridle at filling in forms which merely seek statistical information. What is needed is a simple stance which will enable as much evidence of all kinds as is available to be evaluated. This material will be both what is measureable – numbers, buildings, personnel, and quantifiable activities like services – and what is less conscious – the feelings that members and non-members alike invest in a church. Through such an approach an appreciation of the task of the church, what it actually does, may be reached and, on the basis of this, patterns of training and organization may be established which are relevant to that task and to the permanent responsibility of the church to embody and proclaim the gospel.

Any enterprise may be considered as a whole so long as it is examined with reference to what goes on between it and the environment in which it is set. A factory can be looked at for what it produces from the raw materials it takes in, from the perspective of the way it affects the lives of its employees who pass through on each shift, and from the financial turnover. A school or college may be scrutinized in the same way – its input of students and staff; the process of learning; and its effect upon the world outside its boundaries through the quality of people having it and the standard of research work presented by it. We can do the same with a local church. One facet of its life is worship. This is a churchly activity which provides one means of identifying the church as a distinctive institution among many. It offers people opportunities for worship and is a rallying point at which the members become self-consciously members – worshipping Christians. We would wonder quite what title a church had to be considered a church if it did not worship in some fashion. By examining this characteristic behaviour we may discern the process which occurs in and through the church's activity. The worshippers come with their lives, the turmoil of emotions and pressures of living; in the act of worship all this is given a new orientation; and at the end of the service the changed worshippers return to their daily

4

round. This is not a total description of worship, but it is a simple way of seeing a process in this characteristically churchly activity. It suggests one way in which the church and its environment interact across the boundary between them. This process has to be viewed both in terms of what is obvious (building, service order, people, leaders, followers and the like) and in terms of what is not immediately available to public view (the covert emotional attitudes of the worshippers). Indeed it may also be that the worshipping activity of the local church has some significance even for the non-attender.

The focus of attention, therefore, upon which an interpretation of the Church's task may be based is neither the internal life of the Church nor the world in which it is set. It is rather on the ways, consciously and unconsciously, that the two interact. When such interaction is described we may be able to discern what the Church is actually doing and thus move towards realistic suggestions for developing its ministry. The concept of '*inter*action' is important. for the emphasis in this study is not upon the Church going to the world with whatever it has to offer. Nor is it upon the ways in which the world may come to and hold expectations of the Church. It is particularly upon the way the two interact and have an effect upon each other so as to provide the occasion for and context of Christian ministry.

Three examples of such interaction, each drawn from a very different social and cultural background in England, may clarify the sort of material with which we are dealing. Parish A is an old town onto which a series of overspill urban housing estates has been grafted. It is one parish, in which there is one church building, a vicar and a curate. The church building is on one side of the newly developed town, and for most of the population it is not easy to find. As might be expected there is a high birth rate and parents regularly bring their children for baptism. New population, new local government organization and numerous social stresses all combine to create a lively but struggling town. The congregation at the church is about 400, but the magazine has a circulation of 1000 and it is known that the readership is greater. One woman was interviewed who had no direct connection with the church. She believed that it counted for little in the town. But when it was suggested that the bishop be recommended to remove the vicar and deploy resources elsewhere, she answered seriously, 'Oh no! We are our past, and the church is the only guardian of that past.' She then added, 'It is a comfort to know that the vicar prays for the town and the world.' A teacher graphically described the vicar's job as to bring relief from the fantasies about society. He could not elaborate this, but was struggling to give the vicar a distinct role, which was different from those of teachers or social workers and which was important for the life of the town. This was confirmed by another interviewee, a senior social worker. There were many social problems in the town and a shortage of social workers. She might reasonably have regarded the vicar as a potential ally or ancillary, but for her 'the vicar is a different person. He is not expected to do things, unlike the social services. He should be more dependable.' When pressed on what she meant by 'dependable', she interpreted it as meaning that he should be available but not remote. But she also felt that if he became too active he would become remote, however laudable the works in which he engaged.

There seemed to be a wish that the church should be visible – vicar, magazine, prayers – but not too close. It was useful at points where people in public positions found themselves having to appear assured but where they themselves had inner doubts. Thus in a society in which God seems to play little obvious part, parents struggle to find the church and to have their children baptized; someone who takes no notice of the church feels that prayers ought to be said; others burdened with social problems look for someone to stand with them but just beyond their horizons, as if to give reassurance that the thin line between order and chaos is being held. The church may not necessarily be the only body performing this task. But it is a task which the church is performing.

We may turn to a rural area. In Parish B there has been little disturbance for centuries. The railway brought people to retire there and more recently some commuters have arrived. During the past six years the church building has needed major structural work, first to the roof and then to the tower. To raise very large sums in so small a village was an enormous undertaking. The church was not beautiful enough to attract many visitors; the money had to come from local people. Yet there was little apparent anxiety on the part of those who had to raise it. A deep conviction prevailed that it would be forthcoming. This was not the product of faith on the part of the congregation. It was a profoundly held belief throughout the village. The church was more than the property of the worshipping congregation. The same seemed true of the incumbent. By today's standards the parish is small and it is not surprising to find it on the list for possible amalgamation with other parishes. Yet both members of the congregation and parishioners evidenced a firm conviction that the parish would continue to have its own vicar. The bishop, the archdeacon, the diocesan office and even the pastoral committee were variously claimed to have given a promise of this, although nobody had in fact spoken. It is not difficult today for a congregation to misunderstand a discussion of strategy and deployment. Here, however, the striking feature was the strength of feelings held by the parishioners in general. When such powerful feelings are expressed it would suggest that something very deep had been touched in the village as a whole. The parishioners wished to be assured that they would have a vicar and were determined, even to the extent of generous giving, to keep their church.

As in Parish A, therefore, there are in Parish B, even with only a cursory glance at the general evidence, indications that whatever the vicar and congregation may feel that they are for, the church (in this case both building and vicar) is held by the parishioners to be in some way important in their lives.

It might, however, be argued that although these two parishes are very different in some ways, they are both alike in being predominantly English and the people by professed religion Christian. Parish C is different. It is one of a series of parishes stretching through suburban estates in London which were erected just prior to and just after the Second World War. It is divided by arterial roads. In the older houses the inhabitants are well settled; in the newer part the people are younger, usually with small children. The church buildings – church, halls and vicarage – cluster on a prime site on one of the main roads. Superficially it looks like many another suburban parish. Yet approximately half the parishioners are Jewish. Many arrived as refugees in the 1930s and they now represent the settled part of the community. Jewish children are often the majority in the local schools. Many shops are managed by Jewish families. But the area is now being affected by the arrival of a new wave of immigrants, this time Sikhs. Clearly, then, the parish church here is not the natural focus for the religions of the majority of the parishioners.

Those who identify themselves as Christians might look to the church to defend their real or imagined interests. But although there is a little evidence for this, the vicar's role is much larger. He is in demand, even though he represents a minority religion, as a manager and visitor to the many schools in the parish, none of which is a church school. It seems that it is not so much the representative of the Christian faith as such who is wanted, but someone who offers a notional reassurance about survival. The Jews are occasionally attacked by anti-semitic groups. Their security is also challenged by the new immigrants. These Sikhs, too, as second generation immigrants are needing to find themselves accepted in the community. In such a racially and religiously mixed society the message which the vicar is called upon to embody seems to be that ultimately in this community the believed English virtues of tolerance and acceptance will be sustained. It may not be for nothing that the church is dedicated to St George. And as in Parishes A and B, the parishioners are generous to the church and generally good-willed. It would appear that the wishes of an established group and an immigrant group coincide at the point where both look to the notional English establishment to prove dependable in providing a context within which they might live distinctively yet securely. The indigenous English Christians, the Jews and now the new arrivals, the Sikhs, all seem to be investing something, albeit unconsciously, in the local church and vicar.

These three sketches demonstrate the way in which the existence of the church in any place is not only due to the wishes of the members or to the planning of the diocesan authorities. It is sustained by a continuing interaction between the church and the communities in which it is set. The parishioners focus in it some hopes and fears, often those which lie beneath the level of consciousness. The nature of the interaction is not simple; it is a very complex matter. The clergy and people may be aware of it or they may wish to refuse to acknowledge it. Nevertheless the interaction in some way persists and it is this which forms the ground upon which the task of the church rests. For whatever the church may aim to do, may wish to do, or may feel that it is called by God to do, the fact remains that it is being required to perform this strange task on behalf of the people among whom it is set. A clearer grasp of this task, therefore, should enable the church better to carry out its aims of proclaiming and demonstrating the love and mercy of God.

All discussion about ministry is about this interaction between the Church and the world. In ministry the Church, whether as an institution or through various individuals, meets men and women on their terms. This is the stance which is attributed to Jesus himself as one who came 'not to be served, but to serve and to give his life as a ransom for many' (Mark 10.45). He put himself in the position of those to whom he ministered. The emphasis upon service as self-giving indicates the way in which the surrender of control is of the essence of ministry. It thus contrasts with mission, which is the proclamation of the divine demand for justice, compassion and change in the individual and in society. The two activities are complementary, but they are also distinguishable. Service is more about being done to than about doing.

There has been a tendency in Christian history to transfer ministry from the Church as a whole to specific individuals. It is, however, one of today's theological and practical discoveries that the differentiated ministries of individuals derive from the foundational ministry of the whole Church. This line may be traced theologically from the ministry of

9

Jesus Christ to that of the Church as the body of Christ. There is no longer any need to argue for the primacy of the Church in any approach to thinking about ministry. But when we go further and think of the Church as an institution, its priority in ministry demands further attention. A local church is composed of a number of items – building, members, leaders, structures, activities and the like. Although the church members may regard ministry instinctively as what they do in the locality for other people, it is vital to recognize the place that this environment has in the formation of the church itself. Even before the members of the church do anything that they might describe as ministry, the church is engaged with, or is ministering in, its environment. Although the deep feelings involved may only surface when something startling happens to challenge the normal experience of life, there is evidence that the feelings are present all the time. The church is functioning, whatever it may wish or hope to do, at a level of emotional feeling which is not always obvious nor which can necessarily be understood. Hope seems to be invested in a local church, but often the hope and its expression seem irrational. It is chiefly manifested at points where life and human experience seem potentially beyond control. The intimacy with death which people often assume the clergy to have implies a hope that the uncontrollable ultimate boundary of life can be managed by someone. The level of people's participation in public religion bears little correlation to the degree of their expectation that the church stands competently at points of serious transition and adjustment in the course of life and finally of death.

There is no readily available term for this phenomenon. That which best seems to fit, however, is 'dependence', and this will be used throughout this book in such a value-free sense to describe the interaction between the church and its environment. A similar attitude marks in many cases the relationship between a minister and those among whom he works within the church. This, however, is not in question at this point. It is the larger and more diffuse interaction between the local church and the community in which it ministers that is being described. This description directs our attention to the distinctive task of the Church of England. At one time the church was so integral a part of the social fabric that almost everyone required and expected its ministry. Even now, when the place of religion as an obviously cohesive force in society appears to have diminished, the stance of the Church of England in allowing all a claim on its ministry remains one of its distinctive marks. Aspects of this have been incorporated into the uniquely English establishment. But the weight of that tradition and its awesome legalities need not obscure the simpler underlying notion of unrestricted ministry. The practice of that ministry has rarely, if ever, proved adequate. Consequently there have been those who for a variety of reasons have dissented from it. At times such dissent has only been possible in secret. At other times, however, corporate expressions of dissent have generated other churches. And although issues of doctrine and practice have loomed large and are not in themselves unimportant, it is worth noting that in terms of task – i.e of the interaction with the environment – each of these churches may be perceived as performing a different function. In the case of the Church of England its primary task seems to have little to do with special doctrine or distinctive practice. The variety of approaches to both of these matters which is to be discovered in the Church of England is a constant source of amazement both to its members and to others. What keeps this church in being as a distinctive entity is the task which it performs. This, the basis of its ministry, is to handle competently the dependent expectations of people. Even in a complex society with a proportionally lower level of church attendance, the church and its ministers seem to be expected to stand with and for people at ultimate and transitional boundaries of life and death. The sense of affront when these hopes are dashed, whether by a refused baptism or a demolished church, seems out of all proportion to the level of public association with the church and allegiance to it. It is upon the basic offering of this ministry that the varied activities which the church will quite legitimately wish to engage are founded.

11

NOTES

The large and important theoretical issues which underlie the argument of this chapter are spelled out in Bruce Reed, *The Dynamics of Religion*.

The particular examples of parishes are taken from studies carried out by the author while associated with Chelmsford Cathedral Centre for Research and Training. That in Parish C was aided by a generous grant from the All Saints Educational Trust. Dr Robert Bocock was co-author of that study.

2

A Model of Ministry

All ministry is an engagement between the church and its environment or between a Christian and his neighbour. The precise form that such activity may take is largely shaped by the context. The patterns, for example, of ministry in a series of small rural parishes are bound to differ in many ways from those in an inner city parish or on a suburban housing estate. But ministry may not be thought of merely as a number of instances. For if we are to be able to test and make a sound deployment of the church's human resources, it is vital that we find a way of providing fundamental coherence to the variety of ministries. A model, therefore, is needed upon which the church may determine the various patterns of ministry for the contemporary world and develop its strategies, plans, deployment schemes and training.

The term 'model' is widely used today. It may refer to a standard against which to survey and evaluate evidence. It provides systematically a distinctive way of looking at things. A model of ministry, therefore, which is founded upon the day-to-day experience of the church may both provide coherence and prompt persistent review and systematic scrutiny. Out of this will come new approaches to problems, possibly new patterns of ministry, and, with the continual revaluation of the model itself, managed change.

The minister, as he goes about his job as a representative of the church on the boundary with the rest of society, has a great deal of hope invested in him. He is asked to show dependability and reassurance, while recognising at times that within the church and within himself there is much uncertainty and confusion . . . This means that there is inevitably an element of childlike dependency in the relationship to the church, and thus to its

13

representatives, in that to some extent they are asked to solve the insoluble, cure the incurable, and make reality go away. Ministers of the church then have to receive this dependency. Sometimes they get stuck into a paternalistic posture; sometimes they are able to help their parishioners both to recognise dependency and to discover their own resources and capabilities. But for the church the dependent posture is itself a reality that cannot be made to go away – without it the church as an institution could scarcely exist – so it is something to be constantly worked with.[1]

Two facts stand out in this quotation: the givenness of the context within which ministry is exercised and the powerfulness of the expectations which may be focused in the minister. It may seem to him sometimes that he initiates occasions of ministry. But there still remains the prior question of why he is allowed, and often expected, to make that offer. As for the intense hopes invested in the minister, these are familiar to anyone engaged in public ministry. They are profoundly emotional rather than rational, and usually unconscious. When these are combined with the feelings which the minister himself has as a human being, a welter of confusion is possible. For effective ministry this needs to be disentangled and to enable a critical coherence to be established a model of ministry is required.

There is another important consideration when thinking about a model. Scripture, tradition and theology are normative for the church. They offer evidence of the struggles which Christians have been engaged in when working at ministry. They include the archetypal models of divine ministry, chiefly for the Christian that of Christ himself. Any model of ministry, therefore, will have to bring together the church's present experience and the sources of its authority so that they themselves interact creatively.

The model which is here proposed is best described as a consultancy model of ministry. The word 'consultant' is widely used today in a range of meanings and contexts. But it is difficult to find a better one for the model. The term is used in a particular sense. The familiar consultants are medical, engineering, organizational or management

14

consultants. They are associated with ideas of greater than usual competence, special skill or profounder knowledge than the ordinary practitioners of those disciplines are reckoned to possess. The word 'consultant' in the proposed model of ministry refers more to the idea of an interpreter than to that of an expert. Such a person has skills, but he chiefly uses what he feels and experiences in his role as consultant to offer interpretations to those with whom he is working. Using himself to try and discern what they are doing and what is happening to them, his particular skill is to be able to hold apart what is being put into him from what was already there. He uses himself as a measure and his commitment is to enable those with whom he is working to understand what is happening and then to take their own authority for acting. This he does by offering interpretations which are built upon the evidence both of what all may see and hear and of what he experiences as happening to him. A major skill, therefore, is to be able to hold a point of reference which transcends what is immediate without becoming detached from what is happening. Feelings can be very powerful; the behaviour of a mob is only one example of such forces. The more intensely people share an experience, the more fragmented may become their grasp of a whole view. They then become preoccupied with what seems immediate and therefore important and may lose touch with what they represent and what they are there for. For example, a PCC might forget that it represents a parish and a congregation, or a diocesan synod might forget that it is part of the Church of England. The consultant – or minister – then finds himself having to interpret what is going on by reference to the task of the members of his group – congregation, committee or synod. He shares in himself the feelings of all, but consistently interprets them by relating them to a transcendent point of reference, namely the task.

A person in such a role is vulnerable. He is thrown back upon himself; upon the evidence of what he is feeling as a clue to what may be happening; upon his ability to hold on to the task in hand; upon his skill in interpreting what is happening by consistent reference to the task in hand; upon his articulation of his interpretation so that people might understand it; and upon his continued commitment to being all the time scrutinized by others. He also has to make judgements about when to intervene and how to comment. We may, therefore, say that his authority lies primarily in the truth and perceptiveness of what he says. For it is only in so far as what he says and does resonates with those with whom he is working that they will assign him authority to minister. Ultimately his authority lies in the fact that what he says and does is right. This may sound as though it verges on authoritarianism in a most unchristian way. But when the idea is analysed this is seen not to be so. In taking this stance the minister exposes himself to scrutiny in such a way as to invite mutual exploring of perspectives and evidence. Mere dogmatism is thereby excluded. In addition, such authority is validated by its effect. Change will come about either through people accepting the interpretation and acting upon it or through their falsifying it and thus again acting, but in a different way. There can, therefore, be no room for authoritarianism and the difference between this and authority is emphasized.

This consultancy model of ministry is only new in the way it clarifies the detail of Christian ministry. Although it makes due allowance for the contemporary approaches to understanding human behaviour, it also brings into itself the traditional stances of Scripture and tradition. For it may be seen as a view of the ministry of Jesus or as a description of Christian ministry in any age. But by making such a model explicit, detailed thinking may be given to the appropriate patterns for contemporary ministry. The sheer unfamiliarity of the term 'consultant' in the context of discussions of ministry is valuable in directing attention both to the need for a model and for its significance. It is, for example, preferable to such words as 'servant' or 'enabler'. The former is in danger of becoming a portmanteau word for all and every Christian ministry. It also diverts attention from the interpretative function of ministry to a more generalized notion of caring. The latter, while it has more to commend it, has tended to be used of the minister in relation to the internal life of the congregation, the members of which he enables. It lacks, therefore, the crucial notion of ministry as being both inside and outside the bounds of the church.

The one familiar term which best fits this consultancy model is 'priest'. There are dangers in bringing this forward again. Much that has been recovered about the ministry of the whole Church might seem to be put at risk by a new sacerdotalizing. Many still find the word unacceptable because of the unbiblical way in which it has been applied to human individuals. It also has overtones of clericalism. We seem, therefore, faced with a choice between surrendering the word to those who may wish to retain all or any of these approaches to ministry or trying to reclaim it for the ministry of the Church as a whole. That this latter can be done is shown by the way that the Roman Catholic Church has been able to shift from speaking of 'ministerial priesthood' to 'the priestly ministry'. It is this ministry that is clarified by the notion of the model of ministry and which can be recovered if care is taken. As a first step, since the word 'priest' is so loaded for many, we might use the noun 'priesthood'. This is already well known from the phrase 'a holy priesthood' (1 Peter 2.5/9). Its emphasis upon the ministry of the whole Church and not just of selected individuals is valuable in pointing to the primacy of the ministry of the Church before that of individual ministers. That is wholly in line with the present stress upon the interaction of the Church and society, and in particular between the local church and its environment, as a basic description of ministry.

The consultancy model, therefore, may be called a model of priesthood. It is a ministry first of the church and then derivatively of each member. Its chief components are the total involvement of the church in each situation afresh; its ability to hold a transcendent reference to which people may then relate their fragmentary and incoherent experience; and its awareness that its authority is demonstrated by the accuracy of its interpretations of people's experiences in life. This model, against which all thinking about training and organization may then be developed, may now be explored in the exercise of priesthood.

17

NOTES

1 W. G. Lawrence and E. J. Miller, *The Diocese of Chelmsford: A Preliminary Study of the Organisation of Education and Training in the Context of the Task of Ministry* (London, The Tavistock Institute of Human Relations, 1973). Private circulation.

3

The Institutional Ministry of the Church

The Church no longer seems to occupy as significant a place in English life as it once did. To some churchpeople this is a matter for regret; others welcome it as a freeing of the church from too great a social constraint. But behind both attitudes lies a range of assumptions about the place that the church *ought* to occupy. Measurable criteria are little help. For example, the number of clergy per thousand people is down; the level of income through direct congregational giving and from general responses to appeals is up. There is, therefore, a change. Indeed it would be disturbing and remarkable if there were not. But it is difficult to determine exactly what is the shift. One way of looking at a large question like this is to try and interpret a process or series of major interactions to see if there is any continuing task of the church that may be discerned. The model of ministry being proposed is to be used as a tool for examining practical contemporary issues of ministry. Just as it is designed to draw attention to any interaction which is occurring between the church and its environment, so it may be used somewhat sketchily and speculatively to examine briefly the relationship between today's church and its immediate past. Priesthood today is thereby put into a longer historical context.

In the mid-nineteenth century the nation was chiefly fighting. The empire was being established and protected; commercial revolution was demanding the energies of businessmen and workers alike; intellectually a struggle was progressing against ignorance; and an impressive philanthropic crusade was mounted against social evils. With the nation so enthusiastically taking risks, it is not surprising that it looked to the church for some reassurance about the ultimate dependability of the framework of the world in which such daring could take place. The church responded to this invitation to handle dependence with renewed attention to pastoral ministry. It thus left people free to mobilize other aspects of their lives in the various struggles. There were naturally exceptions, notably in those areas where creative struggle was at its weakest and where the main aim was survival. Thus in the inner cities we find idiosyncratic behaviour on the part of churchpeople, strong dissenting churches, and explicit expressions of fight as in the founding of the Salvation Army and the Church Army. Here the churches took dependence into themselves and led the fight on behalf of the community.

This period ended with the First World War, out of which came a series of hopes that, if aspects of society could be brought together, a new world would result. Internationally this may be seen in the founding of the League of Nations. In England a redefinition of the relationship between church and state was attempted, which culminated in the Enabling Act of 1919. At a social level a profound change took place in the role of women, which might be regarded as one step towards a new style of partnership between men and women in order to create a new hope for all. Throughout this period the Church of England continued to handle basic dependence through its day-to-day ministry. But it also became more self-conscious about its identity, and its activity may be seen more as trying to link, as an entity itself, with other bodies – the nation, other churches in England, and with churches in other lands. Collaboration begins to be seen as the way forward.

During the Second World War fight was once again generated against a common external enemy. The church took a role similar to that which it had previously occupied. Attendances increased. The clergy became temporarily more prominent. But this was only a brief step back. Following that war another major shift took place in society. The welfare state was established to provide all its members with basic security. The fight for survival was, at least in theory, removed. The nationalization programme may also be seen as a way of taking from industry the competitive fight which had hitherto prevailed. People, whether at work or in need, were alike invited to hand over some responsibility for their lives to a dependable state.

Through these phases the church has continued to minister. It may now appear to be more marginal to society, but this may be due less to some sudden deficiency in its gospel than to as yet unclear changes in the environment. Its task seems generally to have been and to remain in the area of handling dependence.

This does not necessarily change when a welfare state is founded which seems to take over this work. For the church has a long experience of operating in such a culture and, if it can act with authority without denying the confusions that such a culture creates, then it may be an agent of change in such a world. The church has offered priesthood to society in a variety of ways, as this overview has suggested. It may often do it inadvertently. The context for today's priestly ministry is new and strange, but the model of ministry provides a way of working effectively and faithfully in it. The three facets of this priesthood – being immersed in the context, holding to a transcendent reference, and lastly offering self-authenticating interpretation – require further exploration.

Being immersed in the context has been fully discussed. Like any other enterprise the church is constituted by a network of relationships, actions and reactions, beliefs and unbeliefs. A visitor to a village will often be asked by people with no public connection with the church's activities whether he has seen 'our church'. In cities, too, the familiarity with which people will lay claim to 'their' church is also remarkable. And what worshippers do turns out to be more representative of others than they may realize. Clergy are amazed at what is widely known about them and the welcome that awaits them, sometimes in the most unlikely places. There is little doubt that the church is caught up in the mind of the community to an extent of which on the whole it remains unaware.

It might seem that the issue of holding a transcendent reference presents no problem for the church. It believes in God. But the experiences being examined here are not

specifically religious, but the ordinary human experiences of
life. When people look to the church their hope seems to be
that it will cope with aspects of ordinary life which are felt to
be unmanageable or incomprehensible. They have some
sense of this rather than of the holy. For example, during a
strike of public employees, people were distressed by the
way that the sick and the poor were treated. But real horror
was expressed when people were unable to bury their dead.
In a television programme on the severe winter in Wales in
January 1982 attention was given to the problems of the
farmers and isolated villagers. But a disproportionate
amount of time was allocated to the problems which the
snow posed for the local undertaker and for people who
could not attend funerals. The church does not have a
monopoly over rituals for the dead. But this is something
which people associate with the church in a way which
suggests that something deep is being touched. This
association creates more difficulties for churchpeople, because it cannot easily be articulated or labelled even
residually Christian, than it does for those who assume that
the church will provide a ministry. Other transitions – birth,
marriage, or some personal crisis – are also handled by ritual
or by pastoral care. The two are not mutually exclusive.
Experiences of life are believed to have a significance which
demands interpretation, and there is persisting evidence
that the church or vicar is expected to be active here. There is
in such ministry both comfort, in the reassurance that these
things can be treated seriously, and the arousal of awe at an
implicit transcendence. The church is asked competently to
hold this tension with the transcendent on behalf of those
who feel unable to do so. Without some such reference point
the church's ministry will appear to be (and in fact will be)
vacuous.

Authority is the third aspect of the priesthood. The days
are past when the church could believe that it exercised
control over the community. Even when its power over life
and death in this world had been removed, it retained some
hold over each soul's future. That too has gone and the
church now has to rely on an internalized authority. The
church's gospel is commended in so far as it interprets

human life in such a way that the interpretation resonates with experience and therefore may be accepted or rejected, but cannot be ignored.

It may appear that all that is being said is that the church is caught up in a dependent culture; that this is as things should be; and that the church should therefore continue to accept all that is expected of it and merely respond to demands. But this is not so. The idea of a dependent culture has a double reference. It describes the prevailing social culture within which the church exists. But it also delineates the specific expectations which are focused in the church and which therefore become both the materials for its ministry and the opportunities for its exercise. This does not imply any form of triumphalism or claim to exclusive rights in this area for the church. Obviously other institutions and bodies also work in this environment. But when we refer to the church's ministry we are describing this task of dealing sensitively and competently with people's largely unconscious and therefore inarticulate expectations. Ordinary though this may seem, it is the stuff of ministry, providing the occasions when a Christian interpretation of life may be offered. An example of how such a ministry may be exercised in an institutional context may make this clearer.

A mayor or chairman of a council often wishes to hold a civic service. Christian belief as such rarely impels the mayor and councillors towards worship. A number of factors may contribute: tradition (which is the hope for continuity and stability); a sense of occasion, which ritualizes the believed unity of the community on behalf of those whose only way of effective action must be through difference, argument and disagreement; and possibly some religious sense that a divine blessing is desirable. The vehicle for these simple manifestations of dependence is the local church. Ministry here will require the church to immerse itself in the feelings of the mayor and councillors, distant though these may seem from the usual perspectives of the Christian community. Then there is the interpretation of these feelings. Several issues arise. There is, for example, the question of power and its limitations. The mayor occupies a range of roles, but the church may be able to offer some illumination of what it means to be first citizen. For example, the ritual of worship may be used as a reference point to consider civic behaviour. Two rituals meet – civic and ecclesiastical. This is an opportunity for mutual critique. In church the mayor kneels along with everyone else. In the rest of his work people pay him respect. This small piece of symbolism may be used to raise issues about the nature of representative functions and of power. There is also the matter of authority. Any authority which the church may have is certainly not in competition with that of the borough council. Self-authenticating authority will lie in the effectiveness with which the church's ministry is exercised in this limited and ritualized context. Ministry is to illuminate the way in which the gospel relates to the experience of the mayor and councillors. Effective ministry is to create within very prescribed limits an occasion for such an encounter. The trend towards such services being taken to churches of various denominations may not only suggest that religion is increasingly being felt to be a personal matter for the person who happens to be mayor. It may also indicate that the Church of England is felt to be failing in its task.

This example should give the lie to any idea that this approach to ministry in a dependent culture is merely reactive. It is possible simply to collude with expectations, but that is not ministry on the model of priesthood. Collusion is to accept dependent behaviour at its face value and to do whatever is asked. The resulting feelings are likely to be ambiguous: warm, because a need would seem to have been met, but uncomfortable because the church's message had not been brought into contact with people. In such a context, as the example has shown, the dominant stance of priesthood is interpretative. Ministering on this model the minister will find in the given context an opportunity for a creative piece of work. It will cease to seem just another problem.

Three important points follow from the fact that priesthood is exercised in a dependent culture. First, one characteristic of this context is the sense of unreality which it encourages. Individuals and institutions are set up to be dependable by those who engage with them. They are therefore assumed to be invulnerable and invested with almost superhuman resource. From the child who believes that father knows and can do everything to the nation which expects its leaders to provide instant solutions to complex problems, the same behaviour is manifested: personal responsibility is surrendered and magic is expected from another. The church is as susceptible to such hopes as any institution, not least because of its members' own dependence. The power of God is believed to be available as resource, so that the church feels that it must be able to accept every expectation and meet every need. One consequence of such collusion is that the church may slide into dealing with all aspects of life which other bodies, for whatever reason, fail to cope with. Under the guise of care or service such activity makes the church think of itself and be thought of by others as a welfare body. The clergy soon then complain that they have become and are treated only as second class social workers. At the same time dependence cannot tolerate uncertainty. As a result the church, and especially the clergy, may find themselves unable to effect any change lest they appear to affront this presumption of certainty. The educational or interpretative stance embodied in the model of ministry offers a way of holding to these realities but of putting such expectations to work in the service of the church's gospel.

Secondly, this approach may assist churchpeople, and particularly those in public positions, to understand the double pressure to be both relevant and more distinctly identifiable. On the one hand there is a wish to engage more deeply with others, whether through evangelism or care; on the other hand there is the persistent pressure to shift towards private, distinctively 'Christian' behaviour and activity. While the ideal is proclaimed that the gospel is for all, there is a practical wish to escape the demands of popular religion or superstition. If, however, the church surrenders itself either to the whims of the community or to the eclecticism of private religion, then the reason for its continued existence becomes obscure. To be effective the church must consistently work with its distinctive gospel within the constraints of its contemporary setting. This

25

interpretative task is often called 'the prophetic ministry'. The prophet is called to challenge false dependencies, but he is not required to remove dependence. That will not go away. It may be immature, such as when people allow things simply to be without trying to take any personal responsibility for them. By contrast it may become mature, when people act upon their own authority, acknowledge the realities of their situation, and live autonomously. The prophet challenges the immature dependence of people, not least that which they invest in God, and invites them to recover the authority which God assigns them. This prophetic vocation, therefore, is one facet of the model of priesthood.

The third question raised by this model is that of the significance of the church's presence and activity for the general welfare of society. The broad and brief survey at the beginning of this chapter suggested that for members of society to be able to direct their energies to change and general welfare the basic dependent needs have to be competently handled. And for a number of reasons, the expectation is that the church will perform this task. As was noted in the earlier examples drawn from three parishes, even in today's pluralistic society, it appeared that the church could and did do just that. This aspect of the way that a religious institution may function has to be borne in mind in any discussion of ministry. For it is here that the unspoken assumptions become important, and unless they are acknowledged, even if they cannot be fully understood, then the way in which the church engages with the community will be potentially less effective than it might be and the opportunity for pursuing the aim of proclaiming the gospel will be diminished.

Various criteria have been proposed to differentiate a church from a sect. In this discussion the difference appears dynamically: a church is consciously prepared to be used symbolically, and at times uncomfortably, on behalf of the society of which it is a part; a sect ministers in similar ways, but primarily to its members. The occasional outbursts, therefore, which are heard today against the Constantinian settlement, are mainly about the perceived task of the contemporary church. For that historical change in the relation between the Christian Church and its society may be regarded as the point when society publicly acknowledged that the Christian Church might so act on its behalf and the Church for its part accepted the role. The judgement whether the Church should or should not perform this task is not one which the Church can make alone. For priesthood is not something that is assumed: it is assigned and accepted. Any change, therefore, has to come through continuing negotiation between the Church and its environment, and that, as has been suggested, itself constitutes ministry. Any repudiation of the Church's task by the Church alone constitutes an affront to people at their most vulnerable. And that seems scarcely consonant with the Christian's fundamental model of priestly ministry, Jesus Christ himself.

4

Folk Religion:
The Acid Test

The representative role of the Church in society is mirrored and often focused in the representative function of the individual minister. From its earliest days the Christian Church has recognized that a range of different ministries sustains its life. Historically much of the argument about ministry has revolved around these ministries rather than that of the Church as a whole. If, however, we now take this ministry of the Church as a starting point for thinking about individual ministries, we may direct our attention away from questions of how such ministries sustain the inner life of the Church towards the prior question of how they are integrated with the Church's task of interaction with its environment. The word 'priest', for example, arouses a whole range of personal sensitivities and theological assumptions, which are highly complex when considered in relation to the internal life of the Christian Church. If we use it here, however, derivatively from the model of ministry as one of priesthood, it becomes clear that the role of 'priest' is not merely generated from within the Church; it is also sustained by elements of the context in which the Church is set. Thus, for example, however enthusiastic a congregation may be to encourage lay people to exercise specific ministries on its behalf, at certain points the community often seems unwilling to sanction that ministry. The vicar is expected. A layman, however enthusiastic, competent and authorized, seems inadequate. Many a curate has discovered that his visit is not as much valued as one by the vicar himself. Some may argue that this is merely a matter of trust: the recognized figure from a known church is intrinsically more trustworthy than a layman, who might easily be a

Mormon or a salesman. But this is itself further evidence for that basic wish for reassurance which has been discussed. When such immature expectation is recognized, it is often described as 'folk religion'. How this is dealt with provides an acid test of how the role of priest is seen and taken up.

Folk religion, or popular, common or implicit religion, is a complex phenomenon. The phrase is used here simply to describe general religious behaviour, some of which (but not necessarily all) looks to the available rituals of the church.

> The Protestant state churches taken on their own have a strikingly similar degree of pull so far as attendance is concerned. Between three and four in every hundred people are attending the state churches of Protestant Europe on any given Sunday. . . The majority of people claim to believe in God, but in varying degrees are rather apathetic towards the specifically Christian doctrines of the church. . . The label 'Christian' is acceptable, but in practice it covers a conformity to the reciprocities of neighbourliness and to a modicum of personal dignity together with a respect for Jesus Christ and for the cosmic overseer of an inexplicable world. This very vague religiosity affects the majority, but firm belief in such specifically Christian doctrines as the resurrection of Christ or personal immortality affects only a minority. . . They engage in 'occasional conformity', which may be going to the carol service or harvest festival, assisting in some social activity of the church, or just paying the church an occasional call from time to time. I should perhaps add that there is also a fair amount of non-Christian belief, comprising a melange of spiritism, interest in paranormal phenomena, determinist and fatalistic notions derived from concepts of destiny or astrology, and a margin of faith in reincarnation. Much of this belongs to the long undertow of pre- and para-Christian superstition and historically it has been locked together with Christianity itself through the magicking of Christian rites.[1]

A priest may cope with this by attempting to deny it. He may refuse to celebrate Christmas, take baptisms or even to conduct funerals for any but members of his congregation. But even this form of response can itself become the focus for a new form of folk religion: some conservative churches, both Evangelical and Catholic, demonstrate a kind of ancestor worship. Yet it is in this difficult context of folk religion that a major aspect of the priest's role is defined. He occupies a boundary between such religion and the Christian faith. In himself he may interpret this as a personal test of whether he will be folk religion's priest or a minister of the gospel. Notions of compromise begin to be considered. He finds himself among those who will not tolerate uncertainty. Instant and familiar responses are demanded. But inside himself he feels very uncertain about how to behave. And where the church has lost confidence in itself as a body which is expected to handle these primitive expectations, the minister is likely to experience these expressions of folk religion as an embarrassment rather than as an opportunity for ministry. When groups of clergy discuss this experience their discomfort is usually expressed in terms of what they find themselves compelled to do against their wishes or inclinations. Yet at the same time they rely to a degree upon their role within the folk religion of the community for their own existence.

We may examine this ministry further by means of an example. One might easily be drawn from a rural parish, where these confusions are often more evident. A more rewarding approach, however, may be to take the material from a less obvious context. This evidence comes from a group of clergy who were working in suburban parishes in London. During their discussions three main concerns emerged. Firstly, they felt that they were living and working where there was no identifiable human community. Each parish imperceptibly merged with the next, and the style of life meant that the parishioners travelled widely in different directions for various purposes – work, schools and leisure activities. So in the absence of an identifiable community the clergy felt that part of their ministry was to create one. This became the dominant motif in planning and designing worship. It also made the issue of church membership acute. There was anxiety about non-believers in the church, since, so it was believed, the Christian purity of the congregation had to be asserted if any distinctively recognizable community was to be created within the parishes. A complementary

30

concern was displayed to maintain a clearly Christian life-style among members of the congregation. Questions of belief and in particular of understanding the Scriptures were considered central. So congregational groups were set up. In the felt absence of any obvious human community they felt obliged to assert the existence of a Christian one.

From this a second area of concern grew. The clergy became aware of a number of major social problems. Questions of morality, especially personal and sexual morality, pressed themselves on them from the wider church, through its synods and reports, and from the locality, through pastoral encounters. From time to time a demand became specific and there seemed to be some expectation (usually articulated in the local press) that the clergy should become effective in 'giving a lead'. Yet they now found themselves in a dilemma. The religious language and concepts which they were using as they tried to build up a Christian community seemed to let them down when they were trying to wrestle with these moral problems. They were additionally bemused by the way in which loyal members of the church refused to share with them in thinking about these matters. They seemed more concerned with preserving a separation between their faith and the demands of life, which were illustrated by these moral and social problems.

Thirdly, there was a sense of dissonance between the requirements of the institution and the intentions of the members. Money raising became a permanent aspect of church life, yet the congregation persistently professed that its sole interaction with the parishioners was evangelistic. The clergy felt caught. On the one hand, the PCC could handle finance – quota, budgeting, percentages, tax relief, etc. On the other hand, the concept of evangelism, which was regularly endorsed, regarded all non-members of the church as 'others'. In addition, the churchpeople often treated the church as an institution, especially the building, as in principle a hindrance to that endeavour.

This is not an unusual story and the way in which unresolved ambiguities were left in the clergy is also familiar. Much of the pressure which they felt seemed to come from within the church. The first set of issues was about the church's identity; the second about the church's private world of religion and how this might be defined; and the third about aims and management. But on examination these apparently internal concerns appear to reflect general issues in the environment. In suburbia one such question is that of belonging. The fragmentation of each person's life and of the communal ideal, which is sometimes described as 'the pluralistic society', raises questions about the nature of personal and corporate identity. If the local church finds itself dealing with such issues in its own life, one notion worth considering might be the extent to which it may be doing this on behalf of the parish. Similarly questions about the quality of life and the way in which religion appears to be a leisure option are preoccupations not of the church alone, but of the parish as a whole. And skilful managing of finance and an accompanying doubt about the reason for this – why the building and institution are maintained – may be as much manifestations of suburban anxiety about life in general as profound theological questions about the nature of the church.

If these questions are experienced from outside the church, then in the central concerns of the congregation may be found indicators of a hitherto unsuspected interaction between that church and its parish. The clergy in this example, as well as generally, found themselves both being sucked into the church and being pulled quite strongly out into the community as symbols of reassurance. This, even in modern suburbia, is the characteristic tension generated by folk religion. It may not appear very folksy, but it is nonetheless the same phenomenon. The priest's role is assigned both from within the church and from outside, and the way that the church may incorporate evidence from its environment, albeit unwittingly, adds to the potential confusion. One result is that to cope with this dilemma some clergy unconsciously work on the principle that people have to be made Christian before the church can deal with them. But in adopting this stance they distance themselves from the demands of folk religion and then, perhaps not surprisingly, wonder at their loss of sense of role and purpose.

Such tension is inevitable and desirable in the practice of ministry. To make such ministry possible, however, large generalized expectations have to be comprehensible. This is an important function of the parochial system. It is, among other things, a way of enabling those in so demanding a role to be consciously aware that their authority, and therefore their responsibilities, are not unbounded. When in 1739 John Wesley remarked, 'I look upon all the world as my parish', the die was cast for a separation of those who thought like him from the Church of England. For whatever the theological, pastoral and personal factors which contributed to the founding of Methodism, the abandonment of the system which enables churches to work in and with the pressures of folk religion implies that this task ceases to be primary. This is not an argument for the parochial system as it is. But the notion of a parish provides the priest in his pressured position with a means of being assured of his authority for being there. At his institution an incumbent is given an enormous and impossible brief – the cure of souls in the parish. He also, however, has the reassurance that this cure is defined. There is a point at which his authority ceases. Being thus assured he may more confidently scrutinize and study to interpret all such evidence as is presented to him – that is, engage in ministry. For this scrutiny always begins with himself, using the question, 'What is happening to me and why?'.

As a representative of God and of the church and as a focus for the confusing welter of feelings which constitute folk religion, the priest has few resources for immediate interpretation beyond this highly personal one. The oscillation of feelings in him is primary evidence for what he is dealing with at any given moment. This apparently self-regarding question becomes the means to effective ministry. Yet clearly if the priest is so to use himself as a measure, some controlling notions are needed. Otherwise the stance may drift into subjectivism and eccentricity. Three principles upon which this ministry is founded are distance, interpretation and integrity.

First, there is distance. Ministry involves being very close to people and groups, sharing their experiences and receiving their expectations. These invested hopes often appear as a wish for magic or for the simple handed down answer to a complicated problem. Folk religion is the cultural expression of this expectation. For it is an aspect of dependency which is seeking ritual expression. In these circumstances it is not unusual for some person with a dominant need to be produced in order to claim the attention of the priest. A weak person may unwittingly be pushed forward to become the object of the vicar's care. People, both church members and others, then look to him to provide immediate and effective remedy. He is expected to spend a disproportionate amount of time with this one person at the expense of the church's task. Intimacy with such powerful feelings is an essential of Christian ministry, but in such a climate the minister also needs to be able to distance himself in order to appreciate what is happening. Distancing is not disowning any involvement with others, nor is it dissociating from them. It is rather being able to hold to a total view of the institution, one's role and the task, and then at the same time to immerse oneself in a wide range of experience and feelings. This is a traditional stance for the priest, who is believed to be able to hold such a distance through prayer and sometimes by acting it out and going on retreat. For the priest, however, when his ministry is viewed in the context of folk religion, this stance is not an occasional luxury but one which is required at each instant of ministry.

The second characteristic of this ministry is the process of interpretation. In order to evaluate the sort of material with which he has to deal the minister becomes both subject and object. Since much of the data comes from his own emotional responses to situations, he needs to be able to think of himself as a measuring instrument. Such understanding will be a continuous process, but certain lines of approach may be indicated. There is training in ways of learning from and through experience. This may increase the minister's sensitivity and competence in managing himself in role. The danger of such learning is that it might be reduced to techniques, which are always likely to fail in the face of complex human behaviour. Particular learning from a discipline also contributes. For the minister pre-eminent among these must be theology. Any serious theological work involves engaging what is within oneself with what is outside. This issue underlies contemporary concerns with the nature of belief as affirmation. The phrase 'doing theology' has gained widespread recognition, with its implications for the autobiographical element in theological work. Being involved in theological thinking, then, necessarily furthers a minister's ability in practical ministry. There is, therefore, no gulf to be bridged between the theologian and the pastor. A third means of checking himself as a measure is available to the minister simply by comparing his experience with that of others. Conversations with colleagues who are adopting the same stance in different contexts can be useful in clarifying what is happening to the minister. This is more than sharing anecdotes; it is a serious mutual critique of professional behaviour.

The third term which was proposed, integrity, is a generalized notion. It represents that for which any Christian minister strives in himself and which others may wish to acknowledge in him. These two facets are both important. It is built into this stance that the minister's activity is and must remain open to the scrutiny of those with whom he is working. To speak of integrity, therefore, is not to suggest that he might be right in every decision that he takes or that his motives are somehow more pure than those of others. Integrity is an applied idea. To possess it is as a matter of policy to invite personal examination of decisions and interpretations to see how coherent they are. He invites others deliberately to seek in themselves how his stance and interpretation resonate with their experience. At best, then, the recognition of his authority will be freely given; at worst, when severe disagreement occurs, the grounds on which it is happening are delineated. And most of the time there will be a process somewhere in between the two.

At the beginning of this chapter it was claimed that the acid test of ministry in the Church of England is provided by folk religion, which is the given with which the church operates. Its insistent pressure for instant and familiar

35

response tends to heighten the awareness in anyone in authority of the dissonance between their own internal feelings and the wishes and expectations of those to whom ministry is offered. In addition, it reminds the priest that he occupies a range of roles and can at times throw him off balance between them, thus generating uncertainty. The fact of folk religion and the way in which the Christian priest also inevitably occupies a role within it thus perpetually reminds him that he occupies a position on the boundary between the church and its environment. Or we might say, he also stands on a felt religious boundary between the Christian faith and expressions of folk religion. If the parishes can recover some sense of this environment, then the Church of England may grasp a more coherent sense of its task, however unglamorous that may at first appear. One outcome would be a recovery of confidence in the role of the parish priest, who would then become better able to understand the nature of the leadership to which he is called.

NOTES

An extended study of folk religion in dynamic terms may be found in Bruce Reed, *The Dynamics of Religion*.

1   David Martin, quoted by B. D. Reed, *The Task of the Church and the Role of the Clergy* (Chelmsford, Chelmsford Cathedral Centre for Research and Training, 1974).

A fascinating study of how a consultant working in an emotionally stressful context may calibrate himself to be effective may be seen in E. J. Miller and G. V. Gwynne, *A Life Apart: A pilot study of residential institutions for the physically handicapped and the young chronic sick* (London, Tavistock Publications, 1972).

5

Leadership in Ministry

Leadership is a key issue in the modern world. It is often claimed that there is a lack of it, as if it were some mysterious substance. Training courses in leadership are offered, although exactly what is meant by it is not clearly defined. Somewhere lurking in the idea there seem to be notions of personal charisma: someone either is a born leader or he is not. This is also an issue for the church and a crucial aspect of ministry and its development.

Three basic approaches to church leadership may be outlined. The hierarchical notion carries associations of legality, tradition and charisma. Obligations to obey are laid upon the followers. A functional view of leadership begins to emerge in more complex societies. As more leaders are needed, so the scope of leadership is limited and defined in terms of competence. On a third view the leader becomes mainly the spokesman of a group or someone who creates the conditions for the group to function. A new image appears of a self-governing group which selects its leaders, whose job is to perform certain tasks for and in the name of the group. The hierarchical notion is inverted. How an organization is conceived determines what its leadership is for. If, for example, the church is thought of in terms of a formal organization, then the leader tends to become the teacher or co-ordinator of activity. When, however, it is viewed as a community of believers, the church's leader becomes one who can clarify mutual relationships (a pastor); who can use the authority of his convictions (a prophet); and who can communicate his experience (a witness or a preacher). These are not separable options. They are welded together, well or badly, in integrated leadership. As the leader integrates in himself the various roles which he has, so he creates some integration in the organization itself.[1]

The key point in this analysis is that leadership appears as a function of the church's task. Since any enterprise continues in so far as it performs its primary task, its leaders must embody that task. To do this requires skills and knowledge, so as to be able to contribute to solving problems. Leadership, therefore, may be thought of as a form of management, although the two ideas are not identical. Management has a more limited sense than leadership. The manager is one who has to get the best out of available resources – money, time, material and people. A leader will have to do all this, but when we think of him we think in particular about someone who has to persuade his followers. In the church, where feelings are both material and resource for handling it, the two notions often become indistinguishable. But there is value in thinking of them separately. Churchpeople are often prepared to discuss leadership, but the application of management to the church arouses instinctive opposition. One reason for this may be that management consistently directs attention to certain facts – the church's human, physical and financial limitations. A second may lie in the dependence with which the church has to work. The demanded omnicompetent person conforms to one of the heroes of English life, the born leader who is highly successful but is almost independent of his environment or his fellows. Infusions of the realism implied by the concept of management are a valuable corrective to this.

Leadership may be exercised at different times and in different contexts by anyone, but it is expected of those who are acknowledged leaders – the professional ministers. For most purposes these are the clergy, but the ministries of deaconesses, accredited lay workers and other authorized people should not be overlooked in the necessary shorthand of 'clergy' in what follows. The adjective 'professional' is important. It is not a description which is lightly accepted in the church and some argue that its use alone indicates a mistaken development. It is used here in a limited significant way, because it illuminates the work of ministry as leadership.

Ministry is an activity of the whole church, clergy and laity together. Within that ministry accredited ministers have particular roles. Clearly they have responsibility for teaching and caring for the people of God, but they also become the focus ... as 'access points' at which members of the community at large may encounter the church and the gospel. They are professionals and comparable with members of other professions... The life of a professional is chiefly characterised by the way in which the person himself and the institution he represents interact. As medicine is often discovered through an encounter with a doctor, or the law through an encounter with a lawyer or policeman, so too the minister embodies the institution he represents. He invests himself personally in his work. For many the church and the gospel are what he is. Whatever his personal abilities or attractiveness, these cannot release him from taking public responsibility for the church. Equally his role will not wholly obscure any personal deficiencies he may have.[2]

Professionalism, then, describes the skill and competence with which the minister embodies the church's task. His is a representative role on the boundary between the church and its environment. 'Boundary' has already been used occasionally. It must now be elaborated, for it is a particularly useful concept for clarifying the nature of leadership.

The church lives by interacting with its context. It is looked to for something, and its work is to take people with their hopes and fears and bring about change through an encounter with the gospel. This process may be viewed as a series of movements or transactions. To disentangle these the concept of boundary is useful. A boundary serves two obvious purposes. First it separates. This enables an institution better to identify itself in terms of what it is doing. It may define what it is, but also what it is not. The enterprise develops its own character and thereby works better in its context. But a second function of a boundary takes us further. For the boundary may not help the church define itself but may also enable it to interpret what it is doing. A boundary thus creates opportunities for interaction between the enterprise and its environment. In the church's case this is ministry.

Two examples taken from outside the church may make this clear. A producing industry (described over-simply) takes in materials, converts them into products, which it sells at a profit. The cycle can then continue. The boundary of this enterprise is not the perimeter fence. If the factory is to continue to function, it must define itself and its task in relation to a larger environment than the merely geographical. Materials must be taken in as and when needed. The demands of the market require a sophisticated response. To handle these and the many other variables which contribute to running a business, the boundary of the enterprise has to be conceived dynamically. It is held in the minds of the people involved in and with the factory and provides a way of examining the negotiation that takes place with the world outside, making sure that it is about things that matter. When it is about peripherals the enterprise fails. If we then think of the same institution not in terms of inert materials but in terms of the people who are caught up in it, their varied personalities and emotions, the regulation of and discernment of the boundary becomes a more delicate, highly personal, but no less crucial, process.

As the second example we may consider the individual. A mature person has a concept of the self as unique. This functions between the inner world of feeling – good, bad and ambivalent – and the outer world. Some transactions are allowed between the two; some are rejected. In this way the individual lives more or less well in the world. The difference between a mature individual and an immature one, such as a baby, lies largely in the extent to which this concept of the self has developed and to which it can be used as a regulator. This self may be viewed as managing the boundary between the inner and outer worlds of the person. This is analogous to an institution. The leader has the job of holding and regulating what happens at these crucial boundaries. He is, in a somewhat crude formulation, the enterprise's self. He occupies the boundary, working with others to discern it; testing how correctly it is perceived; arguing, sometimes fighting, for it; and all the time having to experience in himself the interactions which are happening across it.

If boundaries are wrongly determined, any exercise of control is felt to be inappropriate and confusing. This will be felt not only by the leader, but also by the institution and its environment. There are especially important implications in this for leadership in the church, not least because of the way in which the internal life of the church is in part a reflection of the wider life of the parish (or other immediate context) as a whole. The following illustration demonstrates the point.

This parish is a large village which has two church buildings. Each is of its type interesting. They seem merely to represent a bygone altercation between local families. Successive vicars, however, have been unable to resolve the serious problems that the two churches seem to create, and many members of the congregation seem genuinely mystified by the way in which the question of what to do about them persists. The village itself appears united, but underneath there is a series of unacknowledged divisions between, e.g., the old villagers and the newcomers, the local artisans and commuters, and between tenants and home owners. It is not surprising, therefore, that the existence of two churches becomes more widely significant than some of the church members realize. The life of the church is marked by protestations of unity and violent disagreements, although these are only occasionally public. There are other issues, but this example demonstrates the way in which the internal life of the church may mirror, and even intensify, aspects of its environment. The boundary upon which the vicar works here is not something fixed and which is drawn to establish the church's identity. It is rather to be seen in the way in which the church and the parish are using each other, although this cannot be acknowledged. If the vicar tries to lead without regard for this complex dynamic, he invites continued and profitless argument. If he tries to draw a simple distinction between what goes on in the church and in the parish, he will misplace the boundary for work and thus generate further confusion in both, not to mention the cost to himself.

Because the church's life is thus integral to its context, the concept of leadership as manning the boundary of the church's task is a vital one if there is to be clarity of aim and coherent action. This regulation of the boundary demands that the leader attends both to the environment and to the inner life of the church at the same time. For this inner life has two key facets to it. It provides the resource for ministry, and this has to be managed to the best effect. Human resources are not limitless. It also is a mirror of what is happening in the parish, if looked at with care. It thus also provides material which is to be interpreted as evidence for what the church at any moment is specifically being invited to handle. Bringing this critical discernment of what is happening inside and outside the church together creatively is a basic skill.

Leadership, then, in any enterprise may be thought of as regulating boundaries. In the case of the church such boundaries are particularly difficult to discern because of the continuous interaction which occurs, largely at an unconscious level, between the church and its environment. This is carried on through people who are sometimes part of both and at an emotionally profound level which inhibits any superficial or easy treatment of the issues. The minister as he works on the boundaries is therefore subject to pressures which may manifest themselves insidiously. For example, to express uncertainty may in the church be labelled a crisis of faith. It then becomes difficult for ministers to acknowledge any uncertainty without feeling that they have failed. Yet a moment's reflection will show that uncertainty is necessary in human life. Without the challenge of doubt change cannot be accomplished. And such uncertainty would be typical for a leader in any enterprise that was actively pursuing a significant and demanding task. Pressures, therefore, for certainty, which are endemic in the dependent culture, need constant scrutiny if the minister is not to be diverted from his role and the church from its task. Two major types of pressure upon the leader are discernible.

The first urges the minister to work increasingly from within the church. When he is thus pulled off the boundary with the world, care for the minister's personal boundaries and those of others becomes increasingly a preoccupation. Intimate relationships take priority over the way that the church relates to the community. His role may then become one of enabling the laity to witness. Churches where this happens tend to claim a teaching ministry, in which the Bible is expounded or the Church's traditions explained. These activities become ends in themselves because they create conditions within which personally intense relationships may develop. Opportunities for fellowship and sometimes an informal style of family worship accentuate this tendency. And there is usually an unexamined confusion between worship provided for families and worship by the new family of intimate relations, the congregation. To some these may seem a desirable recovery of a scriptural and soundly traditional view of the church. But they also represent an unconscious response to external demands, which is well illustrated by the concept of an 'every member ministry'.

On a hierarchical view of the church (so runs the argument) the minister leads from the top of the pyramid, the base of which comprises the church members who support him there. An every member ministry inverts the pyramid. The members have a ministry to each other and to the world, while the authorized minister enables this large group to carry the gospel with them on a broad front to the world. The community or society is something with which to deal, but the boundary around the church inadvertently begins to become a barrier. To cross it a person needs either to know the required language or to possess the proper credentials. The congregation itself increasingly becomes an association and loses any sense it may have of representing others. As for the minister, he will on the whole be released from regulating any boundary between the church and its environment, but will increasingly find himself in demand for managing other boundaries, especially those between member and member within the congregation. In this way vicar and congregation may without realizing it collude in meeting each other's needs: the members need the vicar as the teacher upon whom they may rely; the vicar needs the congregation in order to sustain his view of himself as its enabler. Sometimes churches deliberately embrace this approach, although the implications for such a decision for the task of a local parish church are often not considered. Others may drift into it unsuspectingly, as did the vicar of one urban parish (population 15,000), who wrote in his magazine, 'It is very difficult when on one's own to visit all the 150/200 homes in our parish.' 'Parish' had contracted to 'members'.

An alternative response to the pressure upon the boundary may be for the minister to try and escape from the expectations of the congregation and move further into the world outside the church. If the first response was based upon an enabling ministry within the church, the second results in immersion in the structures of society, often at the expense of owning the church. Usually this takes the form of social action, whether through care or a political stance, and education or counselling. The most obvious characteristic of this response is the way in which all boundaries are dissolved. Geographically, for example, parochial or diocesan boundaries are ignored in the interests of a work which, it is believed, requires the minister to roam over them. It was not merely to remove an inconvenience that the church authorities in the film *Heavens Above* finally responded to the vicar's (Peter Sellers) uncritical social gospel by making him bishop of outer space – a boundariless man in a boundariless environment. A parallel tendency is to affirm the relevance and equal importance to the church of everything. There is no boundary to be managed: everything is accepted. The church's caring activity becomes meeting the needs, or presumed needs, of society's casualties. Good works are performed, but the demand for such ministry ultimately proves insatiable. The church is not able to respond to all of them and unless it can acquire new resource, it may run out of energy. Sometimes the minister can find new aid from trusts, local government or national programmes. This for a while allows the belief that all this caring costs the church very little. But, recalling that dependent people persistently believe that work can be accomplished without effort or cost, it may be that when a church claims that what it is doing costs very little, then the activity is in fact irresponsible.

In this situation a further complication arises. The local church may wonder how it is to retain its minister either for his ministry to the church or in terms of his accountability for what he is doing. By contrast the minister may wonder how he can avoid being trapped in the structures. Suspicion, even hostility, may develop. This is largely due to the leader's failure to manage the institution's boundary because he is unable or unwilling to endure and use creatively the uncertainties which that position exposes in him. These are then exchanged for the believed certainty and security from scrutiny of an uncritical, maybe charismatic, semi-nomadic existence in a boundariless environment.

Undoubtedly much useful work may be and is done from each of these responses to pressure. It is worth noting, however, that both stances, the proponents of which are sometimes reduced to disparaging one another – 'fundamentalist' and 'social gospeller' – are responses to an identical experience. And both tend also to encourage a charismatic approach to leadership, in which the person of the leader is central. But the choice does not lie on a spectrum from social action to a form of sacramental or biblical fundamentalism. It is rather between surrendering to this desire for certainty or being able to grasp that the reality of uncertainty is evidence not of a crisis of faith but of potentially effective leadership in task performance.

In intensity of expectation, however, the members of a congregation seem to outdo their neighbours. Even when such feelings are interpreted as evidence for the way in which church and parish are interacting, there seems to be a residuum of inexplicable demand. Many a minister feels that he would be only too pleased to be more occupied on the boundary with the community. In practice, however, the congregation interposes itself. The members' behaviour seems volatile and the slightest miscalculation in handling them seems to engender extraordinary and disproportionate agitation. In the exercise of leadership, therefore, some way is needed of distinguishing between feelings which are evidence for what the church is doing and those which seem to be felt almost for their own sake. These are best described as 'sentience'.

Any group of people is made up of those who are experiencing at least three levels of life. Each member has his private world of thoughts and feelings. He may choose not to communicate them and to a large degree they may be inexpressible. Beyond this world lies the perceived world of time and space which he shares with others. Thirdly, there is the world of shared values and assumptions, fantasies and beliefs, which hold the members together. These things are vital for the group's existence, for without them each member might find he has no reason to belong. In a congregation this last world is partly found in the expressions of the Christian faith (creeds and liturgy) and partly in the particularly way in which things are done. They become points of acute tension when they are challenged. The perceived world which is shared with others consists of things like the building, the times of services, the offertory scheme and the day-to-day paraphernalia of church life. The private world of each member is mostly incommunicable, although it may occasionally be exposed in pastoral contact with the minister or when it produces scandalous public behaviour.

For a church adequately to perfom its task this sentience has to be harnessed to the work. As leader the minister has the job of making the two work in harmony. This is a specially sensitive requirement in bodies like churches and other educational and social institutions. For their task is to handle people and those who make up the membership of the institution are themselves members chiefly because of the extent to which their own emotional needs are being fulfilled. In such circumstances it is likely that the more effective the work at the church's task, the stronger the critical sentience. Members will know that they are being led in such a way that their feelings are being treated seriously and being assigned genuine value. The way to do this is expressly to evaluate them critically in the light of the task in hand. When sentience is thus harnessed to task there is little need to spend much time or effort in consciously fostering fellowship.

The leader, then, monitors the way in which the church is performing its task. To do this he has to be able to perceive changes in the environment and in the church, so that he may be able to interpret the interaction. To be effective, therefore, he must as much as possible be exposed on the interface between the church and its context. It also becomes clear that to try and mobilize church members through friendship or personal loyalty alone will tend to split task from sentience and so leave the church vulnerable to the whims of personal feeling. Attempts, therefore, to exercise leadership which are not related to managing the church's task and which derive from personal relationships and fellowship will have serious consequences: the church's work may not be done and distress and possibly anger will be generated; irrelevant activity will predominate, leading to exhaustion for all; and at the emotional level such turmoil will ensue that it will become itself the preoccupation of the whole enterprise.

Ministry is, therefore, also about effective leadership. This is illuminated by the model of priesthood. And that this practical interpretation of ministry is soundly based upon the prime example of Christ the leader will become further apparent as we turn to examine this model in relation to some traditional concepts of ministry

NOTES

1 This description is taken from J. J. A. Vollebergh, 'Religious Leadership', in Lucas Grollenberg *et al.*, *Minister? Pastor? Prophet?* (ET London, SCM Press, 1980).

2 *The Continuing Education of the Church's Ministers*: GSMisc 122 (London, CIO, 1980), p. 9.

Useful discussions of leadership in terms of task and sentience may be found in Miller and Rice, *Systems of Organisation*.

6
Traditional Concepts Revalued

A question which underlies much of the contemporary discussion about Church and ministry is how the insights which are being discovered through a renewed study of Scripture and of Christian origins may relate to the present realities of church life. Some points of consensus have emerged in those studies. It is widely agreed that the Church's ministry as a whole has priority over that of the ordained ministers. The local church and its practice of ministry is affirmed. A further agreement is that all Christian ministries cannot be contained in the ministry of one person; it is a collaborative activity. These are all points which have already been confirmed in this book. One main difference in stance, which links to the fundamental question of how these new understandings relate to the work of one particular church, needs elaborating.

Throughout this discussion emphasis has been placed on the interaction between the church and its environment as the point of ministry. When this perception is applied to the role of the minister, it follows that the shape or pattern of specific ministries and the way that they are exercised will depend as much upon the task of a particular church as upon any internally generated theological insights. Sometimes the church's own dependence leads it to seek absolute certainty through its historical or scriptural studies. Yet however useful these are, they are necessarily of limited value. For the church cannot, however it might at times wish to, revert to what it believes it was in any previous age. These studies, therefore, provide critical reflection but cannot become prescriptive. Work at any theology of ministry requires that the context in which a church lives is taken as seriously as

48

those critical insights which derive from the study of Scripture, history and tradition.

The aim, therefore, of this chapter is to show how the present approach may illuminate some of the foundational understandings of the Church about ministry. The future of the Church's ministry in a changed and changing world will depend upon its ability to understand itself afresh in every context and to respond confidently in the light of that understanding. The Church's vocation in ministry is to priesthood. This provides a model both of the Church as an institution set in society as well as for the particular ministries exercised by individuals. The exploration of what that means in practice has been conducted in the previous chapters. Now five themes are explored, each of which is about priesthood, but they emerge functionally from the enlarged understanding of leadership which has been presented.

Pastor

The minister is assailed by a range of overt and covert evidence. His personal experience is intimately bound up with the life of the community in which he lives. In order to lead the congregation and minister in the parish, therefore, he needs to develop a stance of self-scrutiny. For this he has to be immersed in people's experience of life yet sufficiently distanced to be able to scrutinize them and to be scrutinized by them. This is a description of the essential function of the minister as pastor. He is invited to assist individuals to manage transitions in their lives. Some of these may be very uncomfortable, as in the case of bereavement or redundancy. Others may be less emotionally intense but no less difficult to interpret. In a complex modern society, for example, a person may be under stress because of the fragmented nature of his experience of life. The pastor's job may be to assist him in integrating himself. But if he tries to do this by some sort of diagnosis of the person's condition, then the pastor merely joins the range of experts and may become another contributor to the sense of chaos. Sometimes out of an understandable wish to be more immediate or relevant a minister might acquire some skills in counselling in order to act in this way. Pastoring, however, is different. As a pastor he would use himself, allowing the person to find in him the gospel and the church. The essence of pastoral ministry is this generosity of self coupled with interpretation. It is noticeable that in the New Testament pastors are always teachers too, and the point becomes explicit in Ephesians 4.11. The motivation for this pastoral ministry will lie in the minister's spiritual resource. Hence in discussing this role an emphasis is customarily placed upon his own spiritual life and on the need for someone to pastor the pastors. Yet important as these ideas may be, they themselves require examination. For if the pastor is to use himself in effective ministry with others, he needs to be in touch with the uncertainties that are in himself and not to be full of assurance. It is the very discomfort and uncertainty that the minister may feel which has to be affirmed for the other person. The more it can be shifted onto those who pastor the pastors, the less effective his ministry will be. For he will have little information and experience to interpret for others, if it is taken away from him under the guise of pastoral care of the clergy. This fact should scarcely come as a surprise to Christians. For if the nature of divine love is letting-be, then to love someone is more a matter of inviting him to scrutinize oneself rather than of diagnosing emotions.

Alter Christus

In a body like the Church, which deals with human beings, the leader on the boundary is likely to have a particularly strong sense of personally embodying the task. This can become so strong that he may be deluded into thinking that he is the only person who grasps it and contributes to its performance. That such assumptions are widespread may be indicated by some of the commonly used phrases about ordination (e.g. 'going into the Church'), which imply that the authorized or ordained ministry and the Church are somehow to be identified. Leadership, however, may be directly connected to the image of Christ as a leader, which is a special part of the tradition of the Epistle to the Hebrews. This clarifies the issue of embodying the task. The author interprets Christ on the model of priesthood, which he explicitly links with Christ as leader. As both the initiator and the supreme exemplar of the faith he so embodies the task to which God calls his people that even when his companions dissent, he is able to sustain it on their behalf and endure the consequent suffering.

This is the aspect of ministry which is perhaps held in the concept of *alter Christus*. This is a dangerous phrase because of the way in which it has been associated with rampant sacerdotalism. The priest was seen as mediator between Christ and the community, holding a power which he can exercise independently of all and which he could never lose. Such a view of ministry is no longer sustainable historically, theologically or psychologically, and it is now widely discarded. Certainly the writer of Hebrews gives no support to such a view. Yet the notion of *alter Christus* may have value if it is used in connection not with thoughts of mediation but of leadership. For it well describes the regulative job of a leader. His linking is not between God and the people of God; but he does have to relate sentience to task. In other words, he is the one who persistently brings the feelings, hopes, expectations and beliefs of the people of God in a place to bear upon their activity in society at large. His spirituality thus becomes a function of the Church.

> There are not only priestly functions or priestly prerogatives; there is also a priestly spirit and a priestly heart – more vital to true reality of priesthood than any mere performance of priestly functions. Now this priestly spirit is not the exclusive possession of the ordained ministry; it is the spirit of the priestly church. But those who are ordained 'priests' are bound to be eminently leaders and representatives of this priestliness of spirit, and they have assigned to them an external sphere and professional duties which constitute a special opportunity.[1]

In himself, therefore, he seeks to embody the Church's spirituality. He also connects it to his role by consistently relating that spirituality to the Church's task. He does not allow it to become an end in itself; he tries to interpret what

51

this experience says about the task at any given moment and how it may be a resource for performing that task. In doing so he potentially exposes himself to pain and suffering, which, it might legitimately be claimed, he experiences both on behalf of the Church and on behalf of the world in which it is ministering. In this limited sense the notion of *alter Christus* might usefully be revalued.

Prophet

Implicit in all that has been said about the model of ministry is the fact that in the end the minister has to risk himself. This is what he does when using himself as a measure, and sometimes he will make this activity explicit in a way which seems not unlike that of the prophet. The marks of a prophet are that he is able to discern what is happening; when necessary to use himself powerfully; and therefore he may be thought of as outlining a potential outcome and thus predicting the future. It is a mark of the classical prophets in the Old Testament that they proclaim that what they see cannot be understood simply as a continuation of what went before. The prophet deals with a present reality in the context of a new horizon, which is how his activity may seem to differ from that of the priest. But this is not necessarily so. Von Rad speaks of the prophets as expelling Israel from the safety of the old saving actions and suddenly shifting the basis of salvation to a future action of God.[2] Such activity is not very different from the model of ministry which has been proposed. For it is an interpretative activity in which the interpreter makes public use of himself. Similarly, for the same reason a prophet will unhesitatingly focus attention upon himself. In the New Testament, too, prophecy is closely linked with witness, and the emphasis remains upon the way in which the witness may use himself to interpret events and produce change. Sometimes such confident use of the self is associated with charisma. But the prophet's authority lies not so much in such charisma as he may possess as in making it available to be examined by others. The essence of witness is not proclaiming but being laid open to investigation. This may lead to the ultimate witness of martyrdom, which is a mark of prophetic status in the early church and is the sense in which Jesus himself might be called a prophet.

Servant

The image of the minister as servant is one which is almost devoid of pejorative overtones. One criticism of the approach being adumbrated here, with its emphasis upon authority, may be that is seems to encourage conservatism or even inadvertently an authoritarian attitude to ministry which contrasts unfavourably with the picture of the servant. Yet the exercise of authority and the image of the servant become mutually illuminating around the question of delegation. Anyone who exercises authority is likely to feel that he has a choice only between authority which is absolute and none at all. If, therefore, he delegates any of his authority he may begin to feel that he has let go completely and abdicated his responsibility. This is especially true in bodies like the Church, in which the members tend to be highly dependent. Delegation requires sophisticated behaviour on the part both of the delegator and the delegate, since it exposes each person's perception of the task. Unexamined differences, not to mention matters of personality and competence, which have hitherto remained hidden, may now produce high levels of anxiety. The delegate may feel things would be better if he received more power and the delegator may feel he should either not have made a move at all or that he should surrender everything and abdicate. Poor delegation will put boundaries, over which work has to be done, at inappropriate places in the organization. The result is that energy is expended on inessentials while important issues are overlooked. This is not merely a question of differing personalities, which is the way in which failures are often explained in the Church. It is one about how the task is perceived and how it is best to be performed. Delegation, then, is a crucial aspect of leadership. Any act of delegation involves a degree of self-surrender, and it is here that the image of the minister as servant is illuminating.

Ideas about serving and the servant are extremely rich and complex in the Christian tradition. Paul, for example, makes service a qualification for leadership and respect (1 Corinthians 16.15f). And whatever the precise history of the development of the diaconate, the idea of service for its own sake is one of the earliest and most formative concepts in the Christian Church. It seems designed to separate leadership from categories of officialdom, rule and dignity. Jesus himself is held as the model of such service. In this way a style of Christian leadership is inculcated which contrasts with that of the rulers of the world. In addition being a servant also involves care for one's neighbour. But there is a third theme to servanthood, that of the ability to delegate and to accept delegation. In Deutero-Isaiah God's servant, whoever precisely he may be, is given a delegated authority to act in a distinctive way on God's behalf to further his purposes. Servanthood thus becomes being delegated authority to further the task. That is how servanthood may be discovered. There is some nervousness in the light of contemporary biblical scholarship about relating ideas about this servant to the person of Jesus. But whatever his understanding of his mission, it is clear that he believed that it had been assigned to him by God for the furtherance of God's purposes. His ability as God's servant to receive delegated authority is confirmed in his disciples (and indeed his audiences generally) by the way in which he in turn is able to delegate responsibility to others. A disciple thus becomes one who both perceives his master's authority and accepts delegation of it. Because he can recognize the authority of another he can recognize his own. The idea of service is implicit here, with its fundamental recognition of the importance of the one served, which is based on confidence in one's own authority to serve. Effective delegation is a primary component of the ministry of the servant.

Priest

Priesthood is directly linked with leadership, as has been discussed, and a shift may usefully occur from ideas of mediation to those of managing boundaries. One such area for attention is that between the emotions and feelings (sentience) of the church members and the Church's task. An appreciation of this brings clarity to the notion that the priest essentially acts on behalf of others. If we concentrate on questions of exactly what he may or may not do for others or how he might do it and attempt to delineate the confines within which such activity may legitimately take place, we soon find ourselves in a complex and probably casuistical world. The focal point in the role of the priest is that he is required and authorized to stand on behalf of others at a point where, for whatever reason, they are, or feel, unable to stand for themselves. He may do this through ritual; it may be representing God for those who find belief difficult; it may be by bringing a third and reconciling position to a conflict between two people or groups.

The connection between liturgical function and pastoral ministry is not casual. The pastor may be asked to hold some reality which the person for whom he is caring cannot at that moment sustain. Obvious examples of this occur in bereavement, where a distressed person may deny some reality about himself or about the one who has died or about the future. Effective pastoring means enabling that person in due course to take back for himself all these aspects of reality and once again become a person who can live in the real world. It would be a failure if the pastor permanently kept these burdens to himself. Similarly in worship the priest has to hold onto certain realities – time, space, liturgy – in such a way that the worshippers can move through the process of worship. His job is not to suspend reality; it is to hold to it in such a way that the worshippers may appropriate it for themselves and base their lives upon it. In this way change is brought about.

On this view of priestly ministry the role of priest is not confined to one authorized minister. It is an aspect of the fundamental priesthood of the Church and can devolve upon anyone according to circumstances. This idea lies behind the ministry described in the parable of the sheep and the goats (Matthew 25.31ff). Here ministers are commended for unwittingly ministering. They are not commended for having done good works alone. Rather they were willing to stand with the needy without becoming at all self-regarding. Their surprise at their welcome is because they had no idea what they had done. The false minister, by contrast, has too great a regard for himself. This may sometimes be due to pride. But it also comes about because he may be so unable to work in his role as priest that he uses every instance of ministry as another opportunity to deal with his own anxieties and not those to whom he is offering ministry. He inverts the process, by effectively requiring them to stand for him at a point where he can no longer sustain himself. Priestly ministry is that which is wholly other regarding, and is therefore defined not by orders or formal authorization so much as by the context of ministry.

The role of the professional minister as priest includes all that has been said. It is not, however, merely this ministry, and certainly is not the same activity with some superior competence or quality. The ordained priest is essentially functioning on behalf of the Church. He occupies a boundary position from which he represents the Church to the world and represents to the Church an example of consistent priestly ministry. The substance of his additional responsibility is the Church. Whereas the layman can exercise a priestly ministry while not having to take much notice of the Church, the ordained priest, as a professional minister, is always also a representative of the Church and therefore cannot disown it. Like any other Christian, but with special intensity because of the demands of the context, he will offer priestly ministry to people. In addition, however, he is also asked to minister as priest to the Church, standing often on its behalf at points where for various reasons the members at any moment cannot stand. Then the various facets of ministry which have been described – pastor, *alter Christus*, prophet, servant and priest – do coalesce. This is the vocation of the professional minister, without whom, therefore, the Church at present could not effectively work at its distinctive task.

NOTES

1 R. C. Moberly, *Ministerial Priesthood* (London, Murray, 1910), p.261.

2 G. von Rad, *Old Testament Theology II* (ET London, SCM, 1962).

7

Reinventing the Wheel

No church can offer its ministry of priesthood unless its organization is reasonably congruent with its task. Otherwise it may crumble at the first genuine scrutiny. The parochial system, it has been earlier suggested, is a good example of how the church may develop, to some degree haphazardly, a structure which is designed to enable it to minister to a large human community rather than merely to its members. There is much talk in today's church about organizational change. Undoubtedly some is desirable, necessary and even urgent. But any development which is based upon presumed aims rather than upon discerned task is likely to increase confusion more than relieve it. It is, therefore, to the way in which the church's task, illuminated by the model of ministry, indicates certain structural consequences that we now turn.

Rural development in Mexico might seem an improbable approach to the problems of the Church of England. But out of work done as consultant to the government of Mexico Eric Miller has clarified four model approaches which apply to the issues before us.

> Reinventing the wheel is not always the profitless exercise it is made out to be. Familiar objects and ideas can be taken too much for granted: the wheel is just a wheel, and one tends to stop thinking about it in terms of a relationship between a surface and a vehicle. Conditions change, so that only through questioning that functional relationship does it become possible to confirm that the wheel really is the most appropriate solution. In this way better wheels are developed and very occasionally quite new relationships are conceived; so the tank or the hovercraft gets invented.[1]

For an old and long established body like the Church sudden new insights into its organization are most probably overlooking some vital evidence. But venerable ideas like the parish, synod, bishop and ministry are like the wheel – occasionally they are worth reinventing.

The first vignette is the top/down model. Local activities and endeavours are viewed as sub-systems of a large national system. The enterprise is directed from the top and works through a series of levels. Although in the church such a structure may be labelled 'hierarchical' and therefore dismissed today, it is still argued for under the guise of new technocratic ideas. For example, a number of reports have argued that some unit like the deanery is needed to complete the scheme from diocese to parish. Along with this may be heard arguments for some kind of line management – bishop, archdeacon, rural dean, parish priest – with a matching scheme of accountability. The second model consists of the bottom/up approach. People in a locality appear to be caught in a cycle of deprivation and their self-confidence needs to be restored. This leads to an emphasis upon education and the claim that aid is not so much a privilege as a right. It may slide towards revolutionary action for its own sake. Similar ideas are sometimes advocated in the church, but the struggle seems generally to be turned not towards the world but upon the church's structures (whether real or imagined). One regular corollary is that such groups find themselves either pushed or fleeing into para-churches, either house churches or other groupings which feel marginal to the church and enjoy the feeling. Enlightened paternalism constitutes the third model. An interdisciplinary team drawn from various agencies makes an intensive study of a region and visits each community in it. They explore the range of options open to the locals and then hold a discussion session with them. The team then returns with its data, selects the most deserving projects, and recommends them to headquarters. Although, as with the previous two models, positive results were discerned, nevertheless the overall tendency was to put the local people into an even more passively dependent posture. This has also been the mark very often of Christian mission, both in England and overseas, and the consequences remain today. A similar dynamic prevails when bishops and others engage in extensive programmes of consultation. The fourth model is called a negotiating model. Here the task is 'to provide resources to help each community to formulate, negotiate and implement its own community development programme'. Even when consultancy is available the local people remain responsible for their own decisions. In addition, the representatives of the agencies in the field, who represent the bodies with resource, have to be assigned to genuine authority rather than act on the assumption that such authority resides only at the centre. This appears to be exactly the intention in the basic church structure of diocese/parish.

Many issues facing the church are exposed by these four models, each of which may be found in current thinking. Questions of organization are constantly before the church, as would be expected of any live institution, but they are usually generated from within as solutions to presented problems. There seems inadequate appreciation of the fact that any significant internal change will only be sustained if consistent changes also occur in the way that the church relates to its environment. The more self-aware a system becomes – especially where it is designed to deal with intangibles, such as people's lives (we might even say 'souls') – the less sensitive it may become at the crucial points at which it may experience itself interacting with the community. Three instances which arise in the modern church will be explored. There is first the question of the parochial system and the authority of the incumbent. This, as has been argued, is a vital issue in relation to the church's task and its performance. Secondly, the rise of synodical government is believed to have confused the role of the bishop, which itself is fundamental in the working system of the church's ministry. Some clarification here, then, is not just an academic problem but an issue which affects how the church ministers. Finally, it may be thought that the parochial system has become idealized and that other ways of ordering the church's ministry have been overlooked. The third instance, therefore, is about the development of a specialized or sector ministry.

NOTES

1 E. J. Miller, 'Open Systems Revisited: A Proposition about Development and Change', in W. G. Lawrence, ed., *Exploring Individual and Organisational Boundaries*, pp.217ff.

8

The Parochial System and the Incumbent's Authority

The Parochial System and the Parish

The parochial system is vilified by some, while others hold that it is the glory of the Church of England. Some see it as a relic from a rural society which has ceased to exist; others believe that it is the most suitable way of organizing the church for its ministry now as ever. The history of the system is of interest, but historical questions have been overtaken by contemporary sociological concerns that treat the parish in a variety of ways. Many current arguments, such as those around the Sheffield figures for the distribution of clergy, focus upon the size of area and the number of population. These are factors in the deployment of the church's resources. But they may obliterate the crucial issue which lay behind the original development of the parochial system. This was designed to enable the church to minister in every recognizable community. It was not, therefore, geographically determined; it was primarily set up for communities of people and their religious needs. Even if parishes may be traced back to pre-Christian Britain, the question at issue was how religious provision could be made for people. Geographical and social boundaries were usually aligned, but it was the dynamic of human communities which was dominant. From time to time such boundaries ossified until they became legally determined barriers. But behind this complicated historical structure there lies a vision of the church's task. Those, therefore, who wish to discard the parochial system or change it on the grounds that it is either out of date or sociologically inappropriate, may be underestimating its institutional importance. This is at least partly because they confuse the parochial system with parishes. Many aspects of actual parishes may be unsuitable for today's church and ministry. But it does not follow from this that the parochial system as a means of organization for the church's ministry is obsolete.

The church's task of handling the dependence in society requires some sort of parochial rather than congregational structure. The latter is about creating identifiable groups of believers and sustaining them. It is essentially a concrete, practical system. It sees itself as firstly of importance to the members, enabling them to be Christians in the world. It, therefore, usually looks like a top/down or bottom/up model. Such churches are generally not a strong focus for the amorphous expectations of people. The parochial system is by contrast less clear. For this is concerned with organizing for a task which is largely in the mind. The church, therefore, performs less easily identifiable functions. In so far as it carries out its task in this area, it is enabled and indeed invited to minister in a wide variety of circumstances to a range of people. If, therefore, internal change in any system is sustainable only if there is consistent change in the way that an institution relates to its environment, any long term adjustment of the parochial system will follow only from a perceived change in the expectations and attitudes of those to whom ministry is offered. Organizing for this task may take the form of enlightened paternalism or a negotiating model. The choice between these two, however, as a pattern for the church's parochial system, immediately brings the organizational issue face to face with that of the authority of the parish priest.

The Parish Priest's Authority

There are three contemporary developments around the question of the parish priest's authority which are worth exploring. This issue is not that of the priest's authority, such as he may have by virtue of being ordained. We are now looking at the organizational facet of authority and examining that which the incumbent or vicar has in the working systems of the church.

First, there is the assertion that some devolution of power

from the diocesan centre is desirable. Consultation between bishops and groups of clergy has become fashionable. Sometimes it seems difficult for anyone to take any decision without first calling a consultation. Communication is given a high priority as a concept, and communications officers are appointed. But when assertions are firmly made and the process of communication becomes a paramount concern, that is often evidence in an organization of confusion about the task and about who has authority. This becomes clear in the church as the number of dignitaries and officers at the centre of the diocese increases. In a genuine concern for communication and greater consultation about policy, the diocesan system may manage to deprive the parish priest of such residual sense of his own authority to minister as he may have. Since the church is handling dependence, it is not surprising that this should also be a hallmark of its own internal life. In such a context, however, the idea of 'needs' has to be watched with care. The so-called needs of others may easily be fabrications of one's own mind. Thus it is possible for the bishop's belief that his clergy need his support to be merely an expression of his own need to be needed. And in a dependent culture the collusion of fantasies about need can become so great that an organization designed explicitly to enable clergy to do their job effectively may actually so increase their anxieties that they may be able to do little or nothing at all.

An example of this may be found in the current emphasis upon the diocesan family. Instead of working as leaders and mobilizing the clergy's sentience to serve the church's task, bishops seem to present a popular model of diocesan life as that of a family. Social events are held to which they invite 'their' clergy; the diocese is treated as an undifferentiated family, complete with 'family purse'; and a chatty magazine replaces any journal for work. Yet the idea of the family is not solely about attitudes or feelings of warmth and belonging. It is also prescribed by size. As the number of dignitaries increases, notionally to meet the needs of the diocesan family, a new diocesan staff of six or eight members appears. This develops its own sentience, which feels and is often described as family like. Not surprisingly that group may support a unified view of the diocese as a family, which is merely a projection of their own. The parish clergy as a result find themselves in an ambivalent position. On the one hand, they will be imbued with a sense that the notion of family is one to be promoted. Family services and similar attempts to express the theme of the church as family will proliferate, but without much thought being given to this in relation to the church's task. On the other hand, they will also find that their own sense of needing to belong to the family (and therefore also of being excluded from it) will become more intense. The incumbent will thus produce more insistent demands for pastoral care, thus confirming the diocesan fantasy about need and diminishing his own authority at the same time. A downward spiral is created, with the result that, for the best of apparent reasons, there is less work at ministry by both bishop and clergy.

A second factor is the incumbent's professionalism. There are questions here of his social significance and status. But more important, and often overlooked, are the dynamic issues of authority. Professionalism has already been discussed in terms of the way authority is held available for scrutiny by others. This is fundamental to any professional role. But if the framework of authority within which the parish priest is located is felt to be diminishing his authority rather than confirming it, obviously he has little to fall back upon. For as a professional his role and his person are closely aligned. One outcome, therefore, may be some attempt at self-destruction. This need not be suicide – killing the person. The professional may be destroyed by other means, such as alcohol abuse or sexual misbehaviour. The breakdown of marriage among the clergy, which is currently causing concern, may at least be in part another example of such self-destruction, which in this case is shifted into the marriage. It is, however, impossible to find any accurate statistics of clerical breakdown and comment is therefore necessarily restrained. But there is a strong impression that an increasing number of clergy are in personal and professional difficulties. The problem immediately calls forth pastoral concern and care. But it may better be seen and handled as an indication of a crisis of professional identity, which may be even more engendered by the church than by anything outside.

The third observation is that if there is a change, whether actual or believed, in the relationship between the bishop and the clergy, the clergy will become less confident in their ability to manage the church's task in the parishes. The professional and social connections between the bishop and the parish priest are becoming closer. Historically they have shared the cure of souls, which the bishop has delegated to the incumbent and in which he rarely, if ever, interferes. Today, however, there is evidence of a mutual wish to make this relationship more intimate. It may be that the incumbent finds his grasp of the parish church's task more blurred, and so he looks hopefully to his bishop for personal interest and support. The bishop (who himself may recently have been a parish priest in this dilemma) responds, sometimes by creating more bishops as a way of making himself more available. He also visits the parish more frequently and enquires how the incumbent is feeling and about his wife and family. The original concept of a shared task thus fades in favour of personal intimacy. This in turn spreads to the congregation, the members of which have a greater expectation that they will meet and know the bishop. Episcopal visits for confirmations and other celebrations become more frequent, and these inadvertently also undermine the parish priest's authority. He becomes less the leader of the church in the parish and more a representative who calls in the true leader, the bishop. In this atmosphere he tends to shift responsibility to any available bishop. But this is a very dangerous spiral for the church's ministry, because it ultimately implies that people cannot be confident in the local church and vicar to handle the deepest feelings of the parishioners. For if on important occasions an outside dignitary, preferably the bishop, is brought in, where lies the authority of the parish priest to handle dependence? During one study a parishioner remarked, 'Our vicar used to be a man who stood between us and God; now he seems only to stand between us and the bishop.' Formerly he stood on the boundary for his people which finally matters. Now he is believed to have handed it to another, possibly more competent, authority. Thus under the guise of a reasonable and apparently desirable state of affairs in which the bishop increasingly meets the parishioners, the task of the church may be inhibited.

The way, therefore, that the parish priest's authority to minister is treated is as important for the work of the church as any restructuring of the parochial system. The tendency to regard him almost as independent of that system may have the effect of leaving him with little sense of role beyond that of meeting the bishop's approval. Since, however, the role and person of the incumbent are so intimately linked, it is not surprising that often crises about his authority are not explored in terms of the working and sentient relationship between him and the bishop but are shifted into structures which are believed to be incomprehensible and unmanageable. But many of the questions about the church's ministry which are today discussed in terms of parishes and deaneries, may well have their origin in the insidious diminution of the assigned and felt authority of the parish priest. For apparently the best possible reasons the worst conceivable outcome may be achieved.

Teams, Groups and Deaneries

It is, nevertheless, clear that there has to be some other means of deploying the limited human resource of the church than by placing one man in each parish until the supply runs out. Two widely adopted approaches are those of teams and groups. The Pastoral Measure (1968) gave these a legal basis, but the movement for team ministry in particular began much earlier. The origins of modern thinking are probably in a statement made in Birmingham in 1958, in which it was argued that the church seemed to be ineffective and the clergy were working with a strong sense of isolation. A new approach to ministry was required which could overcome these two problems in urban areas. The theory behind team ministry is that if the ministers can share mutual support and the use of varied skills, then the church's work may best be furthered. This ministry is not exclusively clerical but collaborative, deploying the various abilities which are to be found among the clergy and lay people of the churches which comprise the team ministry. Yet teams have not become all that their advocates expected. They often seem to produce tension and to drain energy from the work in hand. Some teams appear to survive only by regularly exporting members and importing novelty with new ones.

There seem to be three main reasons why such difficulties occur. The first is to do with authority. The more intense the pressures on the ministry, the more likely this question is to be acute. Teams have often been established where these pressures are most strong, and it is not therefore surprising that teams exemplify the problems of authority. In a team the rector is assigned overall responsibility for managing the work and each team vicar owes his appointment directly to the bishop. However intimately the rector and his existing colleagues are involved in the appointment of new team vicars, these latter still receive their authority, as do incumbents, directly from the bishop. These questions are often dismissed as resolvable through personal goodwill. But that can only disguise them. When the work of ministry is being attempted, they are all too obvious and can be easily exploited.

Secondly, dependence cannot be worked with unless the ministry provides dependability. This is usually sought in a person rather than in a concept. A team, therefore, appears to be unable to present such a reliable figure, except at the cost of itself. Dissension arises among the team members not because of personality variables or theological differences, although these may provide useful and convenient pegs. It occurs because people are offered not one but several ministers of apparently equal authority. Confronted by such variety the parishioners find it necessary to identify the person with whom they have to deal from among several options. The task of the team, then, may become that of dealing with the implications of these selections rather than with the actual expectations of the people. In such circumstances effective ministry may decline into mere reaction to parochial demands, while much energy is expended on this alternative task.

A third reason for problems in teams resides in their unsuitability as a pattern for a stable, continuing institution. One aim in team ministry is to release a variety of gifts in useful ways for the whole ministry of the local church. A team, the members of which contribute different skills to further the task, is ideal for short, explosive bursts of creative energy, such as may be demanded by research to solve a defined problem. But such a model is intrinsically unfitted for the continuing ministry. Team ministry, therefore, is unlikely to be effective as a design for the parochial ministry, however much it may appear to offer congregations. An example of this may be seen in the following remarks about a parish of 18,000 with a staff of three and four church buildings:

> I don't believe there's a snowball's chance in hell of that team . . . liberating within it new energy, new initiatives and new hope. In order to free some of the team for sector ministries we have to avoid their getting swamped by maintenance problems (and the territorial pastorate). If a team has less energy than it has buildings in urban areas, it either has to enlarge the team – and this will probably have to be done by an imaginative use of lay people – or it has to reduce the number of church buildings.[1]

There are undoubtedly many problems in running such a parish. But in this description it is noteworthy that the primary task appears to have become that of maintaining the team ministry, and any questions of the interrelatedness of the church, including buildings, to its parochial environment are obliterated.

One alternative to the team is a group ministry, in which a number of incumbents work together. Groups are usually found in rural areas where a few clergy hold between them a large number of benefices in thinly populated countryside. The aim seems to be to provide small parishes with a more lively professional ministry than might otherwise be possible and to overcome the isolation of the clergy by encouraging mutual support in ministry. Some of the difficulties encountered in team ministries are avoided, but the effect upon the congregations can be strange. Often they meet together from time to time for a special act of worship or some other event. But although the overt intention is to encourage support for one another, these congregations can find themselves in unexpected competition. For example, a regular act of worship which moves round the various churches can after a while degenerate into a form of competition to be better than the last. This is especially true when refreshments are included. Once again, therefore, the clergy may find much of their energy, both physical and emotional, absorbed by the congregations, with the result that ministry to the parishes suffers, not least because the clergy find themselves isolated from that environment by a cocoon of group demands.

One other approach concerns the deanery. This is being increasingly proposed as a valuable unit of ministry. Although details differ considerably from diocese to diocese, there appears to be a trend towards elevating the role of rural dean and urging the deanery to act in some way. Bishops regularly meet with rural deans and it is widely assumed that they are the natural people to be consulted on policies. They are also assigned a powerful position in the diocesan structure as channels of communication. They often profess to resent the chore, but the control that it gives them is undeniable. If teams and groups confuse task with sentience, the use which is sometimes made of deaneries confuses two important working systems – the control, or policy, system and the management, or executive, system. This is a common weakness in the application of the synodical approach to government and it is discussed fully in the next chapter. The deanery, however, whether in terms of the deanery synod or the clergy chapter is not part of the executive system. It does not do things. The chief evidence for the confusion of these two systems may be found in the way the role of rural dean has grown. He seems to find himself bishop's appointee, although often feeling that he is for practical purposes elected by his fellow clergy; archdeacon's deputy; chairman of synod; president of chapter; and provider of ministers during vacancies. One common model which is used to describe this is that he is a sort of middle management. This may allow him to think of himself as having some position between the bishop and the parish priest, but that this is unreal is evidenced by the surprisingly high percentage of parish clergy who are explicitly negative about the deanery structure and the role of rural dean. The structural difficulties which may arise from investing in the deanery as a unit of local ministry will become clearer below. As a potential means of handling the issue of parochial ministry and the parish, however, deanery based approaches seem to ignore the church's task. For they are further instances of internally determined structures which take little or no account of the importance of the context and the interactions with it for the organizational shape of the church.

These three contemporary notions, each of which has its own particular merit, demonstrate the danger of reorganizing the internal structure of the church in order to try and make the church better related to its environment rather than starting from what that relatedness actually is. Any attempt at organization that does not take as its first principle the church's task will prove suspect. Pressure will be particularly felt by those in leadership roles, since they are the most exposed on the boundary between the enterprise and its environment. This is why one avowed aim of teams and groups is to take some burden off the individual priest by providing him with colleagues. But to remove pressure without attempting to understand where it comes from is paradoxically a recipe for increased stress. For the supporting organization will not relate to the expected task of ministry and the corresponding tensions may become intolerable.

One further characteristic of all of these approaches is that they are designed implicitly (and sometimes deliberately) to remove boundaries. So, for example, in a group ministry a number of congregations may from time to time form one worshipping group, membership of which is undifferentiated. Or a team may theoretically be homogenized into 'the ministry' over the whole parish. Each member has to be as acceptable as any other. Parish boundaries, therefore, even if not legally affected, are for practical purposes obliterated. Yet these boundaries, as has been earlier suggested, are more significant than mere lines on a map. For they delimit the bounds of authority as well as the nature of the task. Any redrawing, therefore, by new structures for ministry must take seriously into account these two factors.

The Basic Working Unit

This is not an attempt to provide a blue-print for the Church of England. Such grand designs are usually flawed. It is rather a brief essay in pointing to some of the issues which must be taken into account in any reflection upon the church's structure and attempts to devise organizations.

If the church's task is taken as the key to its structure, then leadership will be located in the nexus of bishop and incumbent. The latter need not necessarily be a parish priest. He may be responsible for a differently shaped unit of ministry. The criterion for such ministry, however, is that it is parochially styled, that is, that the person involved is working in a primary unit at the interface with the environment. The bishop represents such leadership on a different set of boundaries with the world and with the wider church. The institutions involved are not to be measured by size. The population of a parish, for example, is not the basis for deployment of resource any more than there is an optimum number of parishes or clergy to comprise a diocese. A parish and a diocese are conceived in the mind and invested in personally by people. Numbers, therefore, are not a criterion for organization but a management issue. The bishop and the incumbent hold representative roles in these working units. People have expectations of them. This nexus, therefore, is the one around which an organization to handle complicated human feelings will best be created. The fundamental criterion of all planning and pastoral organiz-ation will be the extent to which this link is sustained and deployed in the context of whatever demands the environ-ment is making. In so far as this partnership is held to be paramount, the church's task will be at the forefront of every strategy. There too will be the crucial issue of authority, which by being faced and not obscured can be turned to confident work.

One result of holding to this crucial relationship would be

a careful evaluation of other roles. These will include both the ancient offices, such as that of archdeacon, and many new posts, which tend to proliferate. Immediate responses to necessary demands can cause more confusion than might be expected. A clear example may be found in the recent post of diocesan secretary. Although the various bodies in a diocese – board of finance, synod, committees – may each require secretaries and one person may even serve them all, a diocese is not a corporation which may have a secretary. When the working idea of a diocese, on the boundary of which stands the bishop, is reduced to some notional, but unreal, entity with its own secretary, the church's task is misunderstood and in the interests of organizational simplicity confusion and anxiety are generated.

The Church of England has eschewed ideas of line management. From time to time these are reintroduced by those who are familiar with military or industrial backgrounds. But these are usually ignored and rejected by clergy and people alike. The working relationships in the church are different. If the bishop/parish priest nexus is the focus for work, then, when there are more potential units for ministry than there are personnel available, a system for their deployment is required. Throughout this book an interpretation of the generalized task of the church has been presented. But the specific form that the task takes in each locality also needs recognition. There are two main points to be examined. There is the relationship between the hypothesized general task (which is held as a basic reference point) and the specific task of each local church. Secondly there is a more subtle reflection upon the way in which a number of local churches interrelate. This does not mean how they get on together or what their ecclesiastical differences are. The question is what each church may carry unconsciously on behalf of the others. This is most clear, for example, in the case of a town centre church and those in its penumbra. What exactly this is needs analysing in order that a rational approach to deployment of scarce resources may be apparent to all. The egalitarian assumptions which prevail, while no doubt socially and even morally worthy, have no place in managing a complex task.

For this and similar reflection to take place a means has to be devised whereby the evidence from the local minister can be absorbed by the central policy making bodies. Such immediate evidence cannot come through a line of pastoral committees – diocesan, archdeaconry, deanery, parish – nor from questionnaires and statistics about what he does and what his objectives are. He needs to be debriefed so that experience which is already within him may be interpreted and the interpretation used. This may indicate a distinctive role for archdeacons, which is different from the rather emaciated one that they have at present. Today they tend to move from the centre, whether this be the bishop or the diocesan office, towards the parishes rather than from the experience of the incumbents to the policy making bodies. They are found defending diocesan policies rather than acting as the eyes (though perhaps better on this view the ears) of the bishop. If they are to carry out this activity, they will become listeners and interpreters rather than directors of the parish priest.

A parochial system (which is not to be confused with the current disposition of parishes) is the most suitable form of organization for a church with the task which has been outlined. Naturally if that task is refused, then the pressure for change in the structures will arise within the church. But reorganization which is based upon an assumed aim is going to be set up more in hope than on a sound basis. A parochial style of structure best ensures that authority is both confirmed and comprehensible at the key points where it is exercised. This is the reason for there being diocesan and parochial boundaries. In order, however, to release ministers to work with their authority, particular organization for that is required. Today one focus of issue is how the authority of the minister, especially of the bishop, relates to the consultative system of synodical government. That, therefore, is the subject of the next chapter.

NOTES

1 Peter Croft, *A Primer for Teams* (Loughborough, One, 1979), p.41.

9

The Bishop and the Synod

The introduction of synodical government is sometimes felt to have raised new questions about the bishop's authority. When that is affected, relationships throughout the working systems of the church are also involved. Synodically at all levels the laity are being heard with more persistence than hitherto. The bishop, in order to be the chief teacher, pastor and leader of his diocese (whatever terms are used to cover these ideas), finds that he is expected to consult with others more than his predecessors might have done. During this century a complicated procedure of consultation has grown up, first with the Church Assembly and its derivative structures and more recently with the General Synod and the diocesan and deanery synods. The number of dioceses has also increased, whether formally or informally (as in the case of area systems within a diocese), and more suffragan bishops have been appointed. Both trends are important for the present question, although this does not exhaust their significance. There appears to be a direct link between the new democratic processes and the level of expectation which is focused in the bishop. In diocesan synod he is regularly asked to give a lead and unresolved problems (which are often unresolvable) are left to him and his advisers. A similar pattern of behaviour from time to time is seen in the General Synod's attitude to the House of Bishops.

The synodical system also gives the whole church, and especially the laity, greater legitimate access to the bishop. He may in turn feel that he needs to make himself more available, and one way of doing this is to proliferate the number of bishops. Many, if not most, suffragans seem to have been appointed to assist in meeting the believed demand of the church for episcopal services. At the same time the nature of a dependent culture is such that the more bishops are available, the more will be demanded. The number of bishops, therefore, who are publicly anxious about their roles, whether diocesan or suffragan, is also enlarged. This may produce further tension, both between a diocesan and his suffragan and between the bishop and the synod. When confronted with this many bishops wish to deny vehemently that this is the case. The ease, however, with which they see such problems in other bishops and dioceses suggests that the interpretation is so accurate that it calls forth strong denial.

One useful distinction which may clarify some of the issues is that between a 'control system' and a 'management system'. Every enterprise needs to define its activity, to determine its policy, and to examine what it is doing, in order to ensure that it is working to its task. Provision, therefore, has to be made for discussion and debate in order to make policy. This is the control or policy system, which considers and defines the legitimate range of institutional activities. Work, however, also has to be managed so that aims are achieved. There is, therefore, a further system in which are located the managers or executives. These ensure performance and are held accountable for its consistency and effectiveness in the light of the determined policy. This constitutes the management or executive system, which gets things done. It is probable, of course, especially in a small institution, that people will occupy roles in both systems, but it is vital that they should be clear about which one they are exercising at any moment. These definitions provide a framework within which to examine the relationship of episcopacy to synodical government. There is often pressure for the two systems to be confused. This is due to one obvious facet of any organization, namely that it is made up of human beings. People tend to try and make things work by avoiding the pain of sorting out confusions and relying on personal charm to carry them through. But this rarely works as well as is expected, and a little clarity can be worth a great deal.

Every level of church life seems to proliferate committees and working parties, often with obscure or even undefined briefs. Indeed it is sometimes difficult to perceive why some of these groups exist, until upon examination they turn out to hold strong hidden investment, often very personal, on the part of the members. One way of sustaining such groups is to confuse their authority, and it is noticeable that in the church this is usually done by blurring the distinction between control and management. Two attitudes are often expressed in a synod or council. Speaking as representatives of the church, members surrender responsibility to the bishop or vicar. He is exhorted to give a lead in return for a vague promise that people will follow. Yet the same members will also be heard complaining for themselves that they have no power, that decisions are taken out of their hands, and the council or synod lacks teeth. Here control and management are being confused. It may be obvious that a council, which is a place of debate, discussion and policy setting, is part of the control system. But its wish also to do things suggests that in the church it is more difficult to locate management. This is the case with many voluntary bodies, in which enthusiasts both set policy and carry it out. The working systems, however, of a large amorphous institution like the church in a diocese are more complex and offer many refuges for confusion, not least because the same people – notably the bishop – occupy crucial but different roles in the separate systems. Three such systems can be discerned: an apostolic system, which is concerned with management; a diaconal system which services and supports the former; and a synodical system which makes policy and is therefore a control system.

The apostolic system incorporates the activity of the church in ministry and mission. The primary working units are the diocese and the parishes, which are managed by the bishop and parish priest respectively. This system is affirmed when an incumbent is instituted; the bishop hands the priest 'the cure of souls which is both yours and mine'. A wide range of activities is encompassed, but in so far as these relate to the basic tasks of ministry and spreading the gospel, they may generally be labelled 'apostolic'. The head of this system is the diocesan bishop and his immediate colleague is the parish priest. Any disruption of this partnership by suffragan bishops, archdeacons, rural deans or diocesan officers is likely to contribute to the church's failure to perform its apostolic task. To help him manage this system the bishop may well appoint a number of advisers or directors of parts of the enterprise. They act on his authority and are extensions of facets of his apostolic role. Thus, for example, his director of training may be accountable to him because he represents a delegated aspect of the bishop's teaching role; or his industrial adviser may be an extension of his pastoral role in society. How many such people a bishop employs will depend not on the amount of work that appears to need to be done (which will always seem excessive) but upon the roles that the bishop can perceive as important in himself and which others can affirm.

The diaconal system is about servicing and supporting the apostolic work of the church. It provides stipends and housing, together with the less tangible support which may be required through personnel management. It is chiefly here that the relationship between the bishop and the synod becomes blurred. For finance is important and the idea that he who pays the piper calls the tune will always encourage confusion, unless the task of the institution and its organization are confidently grasped. The archdeacons and the secretariat of the Board of Finance and its sub-departments have their place here. They work to support and service those working in the apostolic system. In general this is also where suffragan bishops, as involved with personnel matters, and rural deans, as deputies for the archdeacon, are located. But the chief officer has been customarily the archdeacon. Many questions surround this role because of bureaucratic developments, but the archdeacons may best be regarded as the bishop's delegated representatives within the diaconal system. For as part of the overall management of the church this system is also headed by the diocesan bishop.

The synodical system may also appear to be headed by the bishop, but this would be misleading. A good deal of confusion and frustration is generated by the church's failure to differentiate between the authority vested in the diocesan synod, of which the bishop is president, and the authority which is the bishop's in his apostolic role.

Synodical government has been devised on a democratic model in order to provide a controlling voice for the formation of policy in the church of the diocese; to scrutinize the way in which that policy is pursued; and to provide and control the funds needed to implement it. In synodical government as it is at present in the Church of England, the expectation appears to be that all synods and the parochial church council will function in similar ways. While there appears to be superficially some logic in this, it is obvious that the deanery synod, for example, in which so much public hope has been invested and in which so much frustration has been generated, will not be able to meet the demand of being part of the control system unless or until the deanery as a unit has a distinctive task. It is inappropriate for a synod to be involved in managing the church's task. Indeed people are likely to become extremely frustrated if this is believed, since not only do they not have that authority, but also the prevailing and underlying feeling is that the bishop or the parish priest ought to be doing this. Ambivalence is then shifted into the bishop. But his roles can be made clear. The management of the diocesan and parochial systems, through which the church primarily fulfils its task, is shared by the bishop with the incumbent; the management of the service systems, he shares with his diocesan staff; the presidency of the synodical system he shares with his vice-presidents. His role therefore is demanding, but neither impossible nor specifically personal. It is a function within the management systems of the church and it may, therefore, often be delegated. When, however, the delegation is unclear or the delegates, especially if they are in episcopal orders themselves, act as if they are unaware of the limitations of their delegation, then the organization may go awry.

Every diocese has a number of boards and committees, some statutory, and their tasks are often poorly differentiated and their authority unclear. When, as is also often the case, membership overlaps, then the room for uncertainty is increased. Any clarification of the way committees and boards are set up may illuminate the boundary between the bishop and the synodical arrangements. The major distinction drawn is between the control and managment functions. Even when these two are sorted out at the diocesan and synodical level, obscurity may arise in diocesan boards, where the members find themselves caught between wishing to act as executives (to do things) and the requirement that they monitor and scrutinize with a view to making policy. If the latter is taken as the work of such boards and committees, then in most instances they will have a place within the control system. One persistent problem is that certain diocesan bodies – notably the Diocesan Education Committee – may have assigned to them a range of both control and management functions. It is not, however, impossible to differentiate these and, by carefully defining the roles and authority of the officers and structuring the committees into a coherent diocesan organization, to clarify such areas of potential confusion.

The bishop also holds a variety of roles and will, therefore, need to be very clear about the role he is in at any given moment. A diocesan synod, as control system, will examine the bishop's proposals for the diocese and agree or reject them. If it approves them it will presumably also be willing to find the necessary resources and at some point examine how adequate the performance has been. The bishop, therefore, as president of the synod presides over the body which may scrutinize his activity in his managerial role within the apostolic and diaconal systems. He may feel so uncomfortable that he may try, with the encouragement of synod members, to blur the sharp edges of these roles through direct appeal to his person. The synod, too, may sometimes wish to deprive the bishop of management of some aspect of the church's work because members feel disgruntled with the policy or upset that they have not been invited (in their judgement) to make a proper contribution. When either of these problems arises, the consequential difficulties will be felt not so much by the bishop and the synod as by the bishop's colleagues in the primary units of the church's work, the parochial clergy. It is, therefore, vital, and indeed the only responsible course of action, that bishops and members of synods should be clear where disagreement belongs and that they should deal with it there, whatever the agony, so that it is not shifted to where it cannot be handled and where it can only debilitate the church's ministry.

A further problematic issue is that of diocesan officers. All appointments to executive function in the management (apostolic and diaconal) system are made by the bishop, and he will assign, and may circumscribe, the person's authority. Some of these officers (for example, a director of education) may have their work watched by a statutory diocesan committee, but no conflict should occur here, if the two systems of control and management are clearly held in mind. Just as the bishop has to assume different roles in various systems, so too may others. A director of education, therefore, may be an adviser to the bishop in his apostolic role, and the bishop may delegate to him some of his responsibility; to be associated with those managing the diaconal system, for example in the question of church schools and buildings; and to be secretary to a committee which functions within the control system. Unless there is a very clear structure, a diocesan officer may use this range of roles to confuse the situation and develop private policies which seem not to be approved by synod but which are assumed, usually falsely, to have the bishop's approval. The diocese is then in danger of moving out of control: the bishop becomes unsure of his authority and is called upon to be personally loyal to 'his man'; and the synod, because it is angry at its own impotence, seeks to deny this by straying illegitimately into the now vacant area of management.

Once again, therefore, the crucial factor is how the church's distinctive task is perceived. From that follows not only the way ministry is exercised but also how organization is set up. But, as with the earlier discussion about the parochial system, it does not follow from this that the *status quo* has to be endorsed. The present systems, however, can be considerably clarified and might serve the church's purposes better than is sometimes realized. Discontent and the wish for radical restructuring are less to do with some supposed inefficiency than with disagreement about the church's task.

NOTES

The language of apostolic, diaconal and synodical systems is taken from some
unpublished work by the Grubb Institute and from Bruce Reed, *The Dynamics of
Religion*, pp.198ff. The terms are not, however, used in precisely the same sense.

10

Integrating Sector Ministries

Specialized, or sector, ministries are commonly believed not to fit well with the diocesan/parochial system which has been discussed. This is partly because of the confusion of parishes with the parochial system, but it goes deeper. For it is also claimed that the church's task in these sectors differs from that in what is often called 'the domestic sector'. We now, therefore, examine how the church may structure a specialized ministry in the light of the grasp of the church's task which has been offered. The sector chosen is industry. This is partly because, by contrast with the older sector ministries in schools and hospitals, industrial chaplaincy is comparatively new and it may, therefore, be less circumscribed by assumptions. But also industry appears to be a context in which a description of ministry in terms handling dependence seems singularly inapplicable. Industrial chaplaincy is also frequently experienced as an organizational irritant in the church.

A variety of views is held about the church's work in industry and the objectives to be entertained. For some the phrases 'industrial chaplaincy' and 'industrial mission' are distinguished in order to identify different approaches to this work; for others they are synonymous. Some regard involvement in industry as a natural extension of pastoral care; others see new scope for exploring a theological contribution to industrial thinking, not only about human relations in industry but also about industrial objectives and philosophy. Pursuit of these aims leads to a questioning of the wisdom and value of emphasizing links with the parish churches because of the unfortunate image they are believed to have. Some again think of mobilizing and making more articulate those Christians who are already in industry; others consider the independent role of the professional

81

minister as a potent factor to be introduced into or developed within the industrial scene.

At the heart of these questions lies uncertainty about the church's task in industrial work. The notion of mission, which is usually used to describe the activity, is fundamentally aggressive. It suggests leaving a secure base for an alien territory with something to communicate which is believed to be important. The personnel engaged in this work, however, are usually called industrial chaplains. Chaplaincy is about care and support. In one study most chaplains described their work in terms which are also customarily used by the parochial clergy. The problems of individuals loomed large; bereavement, redundancy, disability, marriage and the like. Distinctively, however, they stressed how important it was for them to deal with men, who are not so easily encountered in parochial ministry. The chaplains also felt that they were bridging a gap between the church and ordinary people, often defending the church against impressions formed from the behaviour of clergy or the statements of spokesmen. Some found that they gradually were assigned an independent and trusted role so that they could facilitate discussion of industrial problems and on occasion even act as mediators.

Whatever the chaplains claimed, industrial people, both managers and workers, without exception thought that the significant work was the care of individuals. The chaplain in their view could handle in greater depth those areas of a person's problems which were beyond either the union's services or the personnel department's capabilities. To allow this ministry industry needed to be assured of the chaplain's independence, and this was defined by his status as a priest or licensed minister. In one very large factory, where the chaplain felt the need for assistance, spokesmen from the factory could see no good reason for increasing the number of chaplains. The presence of the chaplain itself seemed more significant than the amount of work that might be done. That the chaplain becomes such a focus for emotional rather than rational expectations is confirmed by the anger which can be induced when the church is felt to have taken too long over replacing a chaplain who had left. On one occasion even this was so intense that there was a complete refusal to grant further admission.

The chaplains' experience, by contrast with their aims, matched these expectations. They felt that above all they had to prove reliable and competent. This, like the industrialists' views, is a characteristic of dependence. But in industry such unconscious dependence seems to manifest itself in an acute way. On more than one occasion it was said that a chaplain was needed in a factory or office to cope with death at work, even though no one had ever died there. And every chaplain was initially surprised at the anxiety and resentment that his absence or lateness could generate.

The task, then, is similar to that which has already been outlined for the church in general. The experience of dependence in industry, although it may appear super-ficially to be a curious notion, is intense, both on the part of the industrialists and the chaplains. There is also a high degree of sentience among chaplaincy groups, which appears in a sense of mystique about their ministry and a crusading zeal for change. Organizationally these are two characteristics of a project group, which is assembled for a specific and limited task. Much contemporary industrial and commercial life is organized in such a fashion; a team is created for a special task and then, at least in theory, disbanded. They are often involved in research, and these groups display similarly high degrees of personal commit-ment and mystique as are found in chaplaincy teams. There is a powerful sense of boldness in exploring the unknown and alien environment, which is matched with a camarade-rie which, if harnessed to the task, may further the work. When such a group, however, has succeeded in its aim, there is no further rationale for its continued existence. The degree of sentience, however, being so high, the group tends to blur the boundaries between its original task and what is now believed to be the current task system. Thus, for example, industrial chaplaincy may be instituted in a diocese. The members of the team investigate the ways of acquiring the support of unions and management in order to gain access to industry. In so doing the group has a clear objective and success or failure is easily defined by whether a factory or office opens its doors or not. But there is a major difference between the task of gaining entry and the task of continuing ministry. A confusion of these two produces some of the attitudes which are associated with sector ministries. The members of such teams affirm their special vocation to do what the rest of the church seems to decline to do. They identify themselves over against the church and sometimes appear uninterested in being involved with it. Yet they also regard themselves as prophets to the church, reminding it of a ministry which it ought to be taking up. Yet they might be the first to object if the church as a whole did suddenly take over the ministry which they had pioneered. This is because there seems no means of consolidating the second-phase life of a project group in such a way as to continue the work and cope with the powerful sentient needs of the initial group.

A primary proposition of this book is that internal change in an institution can only be sustained if consistent change also occurs in the way it relates to its environment. Industrial chaplaincy seems to point not to a qualitative change; it is also handling dependence. But it does indicate a quantitative difference; the focusing of life into industrial units to which ministry is offered ensures a new intensity of this expectation. Internally this is matched by the enthusiasm and energy of the chaplains for the project of gaining entry to industry. At the second phase frustration takes over. A messianic or prophetic stance towards the church replaces the energy directed towards the original project. But this does not contribute to organizational coherence. If, however, the chaplains have created a change in the way the church relates to part of its environment, any internal change required will be to integrate this new factor into the church's organization. This is possible. For while the basic working unit of ministry may be the nexus of bishop and parish priest, there is no inhibition upon delegation by either, of aspects of the work. Indeed without some delegation little would be accomplished. A very large factory, for example, might be agreed to be effectively a separate parish to which a chaplain might be licensed. For many smaller industries and offices the authorization of any chaplain is only needed from the person to whom the cure of souls there has been

84

assigned. By thus acknowledging existing task boundaries and assigned authority, all concerned have a ground upon which to make the inevitable tensions and sense of competition work for the church rather than undermine ministry.

This last point also throws light upon the ecumenical dimension to ministry, which is especially vital in some industrial contexts. The church on the whole receives a welcome from industry, but this is counterbalanced by anxieties which are engendered by any lapse on the church's part. The seriousness of this may be underestimated by the church. Industry with its standards of punctuality, consistency, and efficiency, has difficulty in coping with the church's apparently casual approach, especially to the need for continuity of ministry. But above all, however, there is an ambivalence over chaplaincy in terms of the presumed competitiveness of denominations. If one is welcomed, then what of the rest? Do all have to be invited or what are the limits? A factory might be glad of a chaplain, but not of half a dozen peddling different wares. This may be solved by excluding all or by looking for some ecumenical accreditation of the chaplain. Sometimes the whole issue is avoided by assuming that the Church of England alone should and does offer this ministry.

The contribution of members of all churches is equally valuable in this ministry. Indeed, there is good reason for feeling that in the long run, whatever the short term arrangements, industrial chaplaincy can be organized only on an ecumenical basis. Although a major issue in all ecumenical endeavours is where authority resides, this issue is not very problematic in an industrial context. The chaplain simply needs authorization, whatever his own allegiance, to function in the name of all the churches. Obviously he will have the specific sanction of his own church. Other churches may then commission him to act on their behalf also. The principle could be of considerable significance for the ecumenical work of the churches in general. For the issue becomes not how differences can be resolved or mitigated in order to provide a unified ministry or range of beliefs; it is simply that differences need to be recognized for what they are and authorization given for various churches to act towards the outer world on behalf of all. The exercise of authority thus becomes a matter of delegation rather than of competition.

As in the case, therefore, of the parochial system and episcopal and synodical authority the model of ministry provides a coherent perspective from which to handle important organizational issues. It is not merely a model for individual ministers. There has been no attempt in the previous three chapters to offer a blue print. That would be impossible because of the number of variables in every situation. But an approach has been outlined, the basis of which is that the resolution of some of these problems will depend ultimately upon an accurate, if uncomfortable, perception of task and therefore also of role. Without this organizational confusion will merely be compounded with irrelevance.

NOTES

The study referred to was carried out by the author and the late Richard Herrick under the auspices of Chelmsford Cathedral Centre for Research and Training on behalf of the Bishop of Chelmsford.

11

Maintaining Professional Competence

Ministry is carried out by ministers. It is not an abstract concept. However satisfactorily the church's organization may match its task, the ministers who are its human resource need to be competent. Training for both clergy and laity is widely canvassed in the modern church. Dispute arises less about the fact of this need than about the aims of such training and its content. We now, therefore, turn to examine these questions in the light of the model proposed. Although the word 'training' will recur, it is deficient as a description of the process. A better concept is 'development', which is a more comprehensive idea. It links training and education with how ministers are deployed, what structure best embodies the training task, and the variety of ministries – stipendiary clergy, non-stipendiary ministers, accredited lay ministers, deaconesses, readers and local ministries. These varied facets of ministry all relate to each other and the unifying model of ministry assists in clarifying what they are about. The issue of pre-ordination training is omitted. It is not unimportant and the following chapter hints at some consequences for it. But the question before us is how ministers in the church can be sustained in their professional competence.

Organizationally the development of ministry is a diocesan function. Responsibility for ministry lies with the diocesan bishop, on whose authority clergy are ordained and from whom they and other authorized ministers receive their licences. The idea of confirmation as a sort of ordination of the laity, while false in its implication that the ordained ministry is the norm, nevertheless sustains the notion of a diocese in which all ministry, whether ordained

87

or lay, is coherently linked with and through the bishop. In any diocese a complex of approaches will be found. Anglo-catholic views may be contrasted with Evangelical; theological splits may be discerned between orthodox, radicals, liberals and conservatives. There seem at times to be as many opinions on ministry as there are ministers. In addition the claimed authority for what is believed, taught and done may derive from a variety of sources: Church, Bible, Christian tradition, or direct experience of the Spirit. In spite of all this variety, the diocese remains the primary organizational unit through which these approaches in parishes cohere. Therefore, however complicated the notion of a coherent approach to the development of ministry may seem, it is nevertheless essential for the church's ministry.

A bishop sometimes seems caught between sanctioning everything, and thus being indiscriminate, or appearing to exclude from his diocese one or more aspects of the church. This difficulty is more acutely present in a diocesan scheme for the development of ministry. For the task aspect of such a programme is not so easily obscured by the feelings which exist between a bishop and his clergy and people. If a stand is taken on the notional comprehensiveness of the Church of England, both its practice and theology, then relativism or vague generality may seem the only options. However, a scheme can be established which is based upon a shared perception of the church's task – which may differentiate from the adoption of any particular theological or liturgical position – and which therefore may encourage the study of all and every ministry. Without a unifying model attempts to design a diocesan scheme are likely to be haphazard. The unitive aspect of the model will apply to the approach to organization as to the interpretation of evidence. To illustrate this we may review the recent interest in lay training as an instance of one episode in the development of ministry.

The optimism about the role of the laity and their training which prevailed in the 1950s and 1960s has largely evaporated. This is partly natural, since the consolidation of an enterprise usually lacks the excitement of the original phase. Another reason, however, seems to have been that there was an inadequate grasp of the church as an institution, of its realities and of ideas of responsibility for it. To some degree people define themselves by what they are not as much as by what they profess to be. In the church, with its distinction between laity and clergy (a division which does not disappear, however the different ministries of each are regarded as complementary), lay is not-ordained and *vice versa*. So as the role of the clergy changes, or is believed to change, so that of the laity is bound to be affected. This change, however, is not merely one of role. It is, as has been discussed, to do with the priest's authority. Where there is such uncertainty, parallel questioning on the part of the laity will ensue about their authority as Christians. This causes in part the current polarizing of views on what is lay ministry. At one pole the desire is expressed for a quasi-clerical role. Training then becomes the acquisition of knowledge and techniques. The other pole is the view that the laity constitute the church in the world and that lay development has little or nothing to do with their role as church members.

This issue of lay authority was the focus in an approach to lay training which was known as the Parish Life Conference. This consisted of six representatives from each of six parishes, who met for a weekend. The programme included discussions with report back, input and Bible study, as well as a case study. The theoretical base was that adults learn by reflecting on and evaluating their experience. The primary theological content was already present in the members; the events were designed to bring this out and employ it. Each group left the conference with a statement of what it proposed to do when it returned to its parish church. The programme has not continued. One reason was that it assumed that the clergy were more able as continuing lay trainers in the parishes than they in fact were. Recent efforts at similar learning have suggested that the laity now possess less latent theological understanding than in the 1950s, which may be a result of different stances on the education of children and of the transformation of worship with the new liturgies. The conferences, however, made clear that the fundamental issue for laity, as much as for clergy, is that of authority. What authority does the Christian possess in any situation to speak for God? What authority does the Bible carry? What is the nature of the believer's authority not only for his faith but also for his doubts? And how can this be used not so much in the service of the church as of the Kingdom of God?

Three general consequences may be drawn from this episode. First, the emphasis on learning by experience points to the two contexts in which the conference member lives – the conference and life outside. What occurs in the conference may reflect aspects of life. There is, however, a particular danger in a short conference of this type that it might, because of its concern with its own process, be able to avoid facing realities which are important outside. Chief among these was the absence of the clergy. If they had been present the conferences would have been different. Certainly it would have been very difficult, if not impossible, for people to own their doubts and faith in front of their vicar. Other events, therefore, were designed for the clergy, and these became more successful than those for the laity. The studies, however, even when the clergy were present only in the member's minds, implied such a division between clergy and laity that the opportunities for projection were very great. However good the staff were at interpreting this, the problem could not be overcome. Ultimately, in spite of the opportunity, lay people were not able to investigate and question their theology.

A second issue was also to do with how the gospel was understood. That it is to be related to life is the theme of countless sermons and conferences. There follows, however, a tendency to relativize the experience of the gospel. When experience is assigned its own value, it may sometimes seem that the gospel has to be adjusted to the context in which that experience is felt. Issues about its content then decline in importance. It is either considered obvious, taken for granted and no deviation is allowed. Or it is virtually disregarded. The emphasis upon experience in applied theological learning has tended to diminish the amount of critical reflection upon content. As a result the content is assumed, however deficient knowledge of it may be, and the experience of relating to others in the light of this assumed gospel becomes central. There is, however, another and more desirable option, whereby the experience of this process may then be taken up as a means of critical reflection upon the gospel itself. This in itself could become a major contribution to theology.

The third area is that of explanation. An important process in lay training is the interpretation of what is believed through the evidence of the way people behave. But the difference between explanation and explaining away may sometimes feel minimal. Conferences rarely set out to explain away difficulties; indeed the reverse is usually the case. But the effect seems sometimes to be that explanation is believed to remove the issue rather than provide a way into it more deeply. If the problem is severe, however, – as they always are where questions of faith and doubt arise – any explaining away is bound to be only temporary. Study then seems to be a waste of time and people do not take it up.

Although the example has been taken from one major attempt at a lay training programme, the issues – the relationship between the conference and life; the relativizing of the gospel; and explanation experienced as explaining away – are common to any training programme. If, therefore, an effective design is to be established, some grasp of the learning process is important, and it has to be linked to the model of ministry which is informing our thinking on development. One interpretation which is very illuminating is that offered by Barry Palmer. He outlines three processes in learning. First is learning for survival, as the individual sorts himself out into any new environment. This consists of instinctive and usually instantaneous response. A second stage is learning for development, as the learner begins to organize himself on the basis of the first level to do something. This learning is self-directed. The third stage builds on the previous two: 'These processes are those by which habitual responses, and the unconscious fantasies upon which they are based, are brought back within the domain of conscious scrutiny and criticism and revalued.' Such learning leads to change and is described as learning for freedom.[1]

This theory throws much light on the development of ministry. Learning for survival in church comes about through teaching, preaching and worship. It builds in a framework for living, and is the level which preoccupies churchpeople. Learning for development is where much present-day training is located. Adults are invited to explore their assumed beliefs and experiences in the light of the context in which they live. There is value in this and the immediate outcome may sometimes be renewed action or a new perspective. What may be overlooked, however, is that the results of such learning are themselves necessarily provisional. Yet such has been the wonder at the new learning, that often the products are not left open to revision and they become inflexible. The third area of learning seems rarely reached in programmes for ministerial development, although it really describes the function of theological thinking. For theological reflection is the conscious process of criticism of interpreted experience. In addition, and in some ways more importantly, it is also the means whereby the Christian tradition, using this to describe the process of handing on the faith from generation to generation, is itself interpreted and reinterpreted. Service, or ministry, thus becomes freedom.

A third criterion for the development of ministry in addition to a congruent organization and a coherent theory of learning is the need for selection. This procedure goes usually under the heading of vocation, which describes not so much the wish of a motivated individual as the confirming decision of the church in acknowledging God's call and symbolizing this by the imposition of hands or some other ritual. Today there are many different authorized ministries which contribute to a sense of confusion. So many titles and such similar activities, parallel training and strong personal investment in differences, not to mention the varied expectations which are held of these ministries, all contribute to the idea that somehow they merge into an undifferentiated lump called 'ministry'. To separate ministries by status is no longer possible and is in any case theologically indefensible. If we start from functions or activities we are soon caught by the overlap between what various ministers do and are, because for those involved to be a minister is to be more than a functionary. The concept of vocation, however, provides a way forward.

The second collect for Good Friday in the Book of Common Prayer includes the phrase 'each in his vocation and ministry' This may merely be a pleonasm, but it is suggestive. Although priesthood is the model of all Christian ministry, everyone also has their vocation, which includes selection. It is not possible to argue much about or deny every Christian's ministry as a servant of God. But that one has a vocation to a particular office is a matter for examination and selection. The same pattern applies to development; the generic concept of ministry underlies all training, but the differentiated functions which are exercised as a result of different vocations have then to be separated. When, however, vocation and ministry are confused, it is implied that all Christians must learn together without differentiation. The outcome can be confusion. For the development of ministry will concentrate on the roles that people occupy and that means a focus on vocation. Here too the rationale for the different ministries becomes examinable. But if they are merged into one before the study begins, the participants will not face the struggle for an interpretation of what is being particularly expected of them. If, however, vocation is taken seriously, suitable opportunities for development can be devised. Some will be appropriate for members of several or indeed all the different ministries. But this does not imply that the boundaries between them are dissolved. From this view of vocation two practical reflections follow.

Most development of ministry will be attempted on the spot where ministry is being exercised. The parish priest may be the local teacher, but it does not follow that he himself has to do the teaching. Just as the bishop, as chief teacher of the faith, can often best act through competent delegation, so too the local priest may delegate his function to capable people in the parish or to diocesan colleagues. In passing, the nature of this delegation to diocesan staff is worth noting. Although they are authorized by the bishop to work on his behalf, they need similar authorization from the parish priest when they come to a parish. Thus there need be no breakdown in the basic structure of authority between the bishop and the incumbent. It may, therefore, be as, if not more, important to enable clergy to understand the authority structure as to train them as teachers. The task may at least get done, since they will be more willing to delegate to lay people, diocesan staff and other resources. There will then be less reason to take people from the parishes for this work and they may thus remain in touch with the realities of their situation. The danger of fantasy, which is often present in short events away from the parish, will then be diminished. Similar criteria apply to the professional ministers. The basic development programme would seem best offered where ministry (for example, priesthood) and vocation (for example, being an incumbent) meet. Consultancy at this point, if offered on the consultancy model of ministry, would provide the best opportunity for basic learning in ministry. On this foundation of continuing learning other distinctive opportunities for all ministers can be grounded. These will be amplified in the next chapter.

A second aspect of the concept of vocation concerns the attitude to training. While a sense of Christian ministry may provide the basic motivation for worship and reflection (which is learning for survival), a specific understanding of vocation provides the basis for genuine learning for development and ultimately for freedom. Since these are phases of learning in which the individual has to take up responsibility on his own behalf, one corollary is that the autonomy of the individual and the freedom that is his within his vocation must be acknowledged. There is today increasing pressure to make participation in training programmes compulsory, especially for the clergy but also in some parishes for lay people. But it is impossible to force exploration of a person's fundamental beliefs. At a more practical level such evidence as there is from the most widespread compulsory programme – post-ordination training – suggests that compulsion may prove counter-productive. Instead of assisting the newly ordained or licensed to come to terms with their new experiences and the novel demands of the parish and bringing to this a theological assessment, it appears in many cases to reinforce the various conservatisms with which they entered the ordained ministry. There may also be a suspicion that the presence of a few clergy undergoing compulsory training, especially when they are juniors, may allow others to avoid the issue for themselves. Thus opportunities for development must be seen to justify themselves by their integrity and significance alone.

When we turn to consider the content of a diocesan programme for the development of ministry, the value of a model of ministry again becomes apparent. A bewildering array of opportunities is promoted in the church, each of which contains presuppositions about the nature and task of the church. Three general approaches may, however, be discerned.

Firstly, a spiritual approach is urged as the ground of all training. This may appear as a straightforward demand for more prayer, meditation or Bible study. Learning in spirituality, however, is primarily a matter of formation, which, in the categories offered above, is learning for survival. It is vital, but is only a basis for further growth. Recall to this may be a form of regression by which participants seek to avoid painful issues of self-scrutiny and any possibility of catastrophic change. Within church life this approach has a superficial legitimacy. No one is sufficiently adept spiritually to be able to claim that it is not for him. There are, however, other issues which have to be pursued if the church is to work at all. It is interesting to note that its proponents claim that this approach is concerned with distinctively Christian activity and therefore it is the appropriate one on which to focus. Yet this stance, with its tendency to emphasize a shared world of private experience, is more in tune with the contemporary pressure towards treating important issues as merely private concerns than the participants sometimes recognize.

A second approach may be characterized as that of a social gospel. This assumes that the church could and should organize social and political programmes, sometimes national, but often international. Training includes study of issues such as the Third World or South Africa and questions of economics, food and resources. The focus is upon the major moral, social, political and economic problems of the day. A message is conveyed that the local congregation and the individual Christian are of little importance unless they can stretch their consciousness to embrace the world. If the spiritual approach makes barriers out of the church's boundaries, the social gospel seems to press for the dissolution of any boundary whatsoever. These great issues are vital for the church, but some reciprocity is required between the context of the Christian's experience and the larger world. An approach which simply presents new and often controversial horizons may inadvertently imply that a person's immediate environment is either defective or unimportant. For Christians, as for any human beings, the outcome of such unmanaged disturbance is likely to be further introspection, which is precisely the opposite of what was intended.

A therapeutically oriented view forms the third general approach. The church is thought of as concerned to promote the individual's self-awareness. This may involve discussion about the various interpretations of the human being which are currently in vogue. Sensitivity training often plays a part. Psychology and experiential learning are important components of the programme, but the aim is difficult to see. For a preoccupation seems to grow around the person and his welfare. The courses thus tend also to become therapeutic for the participants and their educational value is unclear. It is not, therefore, surprising that the product can be that the individual becomes caught up in various counselling agencies or that a church moves towards becoming a counselling service. The idea of pastoral care shifts towards therapy.

Each of these general approaches contributes something valuable to total programme for the development of ministry. But once more we are faced with the question of what criteria are to be used to select from the plethora of options. For without some selection the opportunities for training will present such a random series of messages about ministry that they will only increase the confusion of the already confused. It is here that the model proves crucial. It indicates that those whose ministry is conceived in relation to the church's task, whatever their particular role within the church, will be assisted by learning in three main areas.

The first is theology. Those who profess to believe the

gospel will need and wish to increase their grasp of it, its content and its implications. There is the matter of basic knowledge. Clergy and laity often seem ignorant of the foundational story of the Christian faith. They have to keep in touch with recent thinking in areas of traditional theological study, and this becomes more difficult as books become more expensive and more scarce. But people also need to understand and lay hold of what they already have. This is the theological process of thinking from experience and knowledge as this resides in the individual and the group. Theology also offers a reference framework within which the believer's experience of himself and the world around him may be held. This coherence is not a container, but is itself a continuing process of confident handling of the evidence, whatever its origin. The aim is that the gospel might become so part of each person and congregation that instead of pointing away from themselves to Bible, Church or tradition, they will be able to operate within their own sphere of life upon a self-evident and self-authenticating authority which comes from within and which others may therefore explore in them. A high level of sophistication is required of any programme which offers opportunities for theological learning.

The second area concerns context. Throughout this book it has been argued that the Church of England occupies a distinctive place in society. The dynamic interpretation of the way in which the church and society interact has been outlined. Those who minister in such dependence will have to be aware of it and of the hopes which are invested in them, if they are to work with the gospel and not merely succumb to pressure. This is specially important for the clergy as leaders of local congregations, but it is also necessary for all who wish to understand themselves, their gospel and their behaviour and activity. Therefore opportunities to explore questions of leadership and authority would come high on the list of priorities for any training programme. Indeed it might well be that these could provide a way into questions of social concern, whether of the local community relations or more widely in the world at large. Every Christian minister should be aware that he evokes some response by his mere existence. He should then better comprehend what is happening to him, so that he may confidently and competently respond where demand is located rather than collude with fantasy.

The third general area is that of sensitivity. Since human beings are the main material with which God has asked the Church to work, there is much to be said for providing occasions, especially for church leaders, to learn about the human person. A deep awareness and understanding of people, without succumbing to the temptation to become therapists, is invaluable for ministry. There is, however, a need to avoid allowing some form of self-awareness to become a substitute for the gospel or grasping at areas of fringe psychology as a means of avoiding the rigours of detailed study in this field.

Because these three areas of study have been delineated it does not follow that they are separable or in some sort of competition for primacy in a training programme. In creating a programme based upon a unifying model of ministry, an integrated approach to learning is essential. This integration is the function of theology. For theology, if it is to be that integrative science which is its sole claim to significance, will naturally be tied up with all and each of these aspects of study.

The urgent and creative questions which are truly theological and require to be taken into account in the pursuit of theology, cannot be discerned primarily from within the practices of theology but must be picked up by careful attention to the urgencies of contemporary human living. This theological requirement does not necessarily imply that these urgencies of human living should be accepted uncritically in the terms in which they are presented. Any theology, gospel or faith which is dynamically rather than literally in continuity with those which are reflected in the bible and the various attempts at reformation in the Christian traditions would seem to require a considerable element of 'going against the stream'. What is implied, however, is that there cannot be a 'standing out' of trends and happenings in society which supports any effective presentation of the gospel unless there is a very deep and sustained 'standing in'.[2]

Such a theology is integrative and is the natural and necessary foundation of a development programme which is founded on the model of ministry.

NOTES

1 Barry Palmer, 'Learning and the Group Experience', in W. G. Lawrence, ed., *Exploring Individual and Organisational Boundaries*, pp.169ff.

2 David Jenkins, *Theology* 80 (September 1977), p.323.

12

A Structure and Programme for Learning

An essay in applied theology should become severely practical. In this final chapter, therefore, an outline is presented of how the foregoing reflections on ministry, its organization and training, come together in a diocesan programme. This has two components: a diocesan structure to further the development of ministry and the design of a programme.

A Diocesan Structure

The bishop's role as teacher is the corner-stone of the development of ministry in a diocese. Any structure, therefore, must take full account of this, so that the essential working partnership of bishop and clergy will be affirmed as much by the structure as by anything that may be said. For the bishop's role in this regard is a model for the role of the clergy in encouraging collaborative ministry between them and the lay people in the churches. The bishop's role in this partnership has two facets. He manages the boundary between the church in the diocese and the wider church. In developing ministry this particularly means the world of theological reflection, how ministry is taking shape in other dioceses and throughout the world, and new approaches to education and learning. The second facet within the diocese is that the bishop is ultimately responsible for ministry, however much of this he may delegate to colleagues. Any structure for the development of ministry must take into account both the external and internal aspects of this episcopal role.

A consultative body to help the bishop formulate policy

for ministry in his diocese in the context of the wider church and world is advisable. Membership would be drawn from those, both within and outside the diocese, with expertise in the specific issue requiring decision. The group would be under the direct chairmanship of the bishop, since it would be intimately involved with his leadership of the diocese. That, however, would be the only fixed aspect of membership. For as a project group it would be composed of different members each time it was formed, and when its advice was given it would dissolve. The reason for summoning such a body might lie in new developments outside the diocese of which the bishop felt that he had to take note. Equally pressure might arise within the diocese for some sort of change, which he would then feel he needed to examine with reference to the wider experience of the church. In this way the bishop's leadership in ministry would be safeguarded and the diocese would remain alive to new and important ideas.

The second facet of the bishop's role concerns what was done under his authority in his diocese. Here the work would be almost wholly delegated. Most dioceses have directors of training and adult education officers. These appointments have largely depended upon personal contacts between the bishop and the officer. Sometimes this seems to have encouraged maverick behaviour by officers who roam the diocese stimulating various activities. There is value in such idiosyncrasy, but often it is felt to be, and at times may actually be, counterproductive to the basic ministry which the clergy are engaged in with bishop and laity. If, however, the bishop has a policy for training and ministry, he can then appoint a director of training who is responsible for its implementation. When the bishop delegates such executive authority, some control system is also needed. Technically in this case it is the bishop himself, but it would be difficult, if not impossible, for him to act as such. For the work which a director initiates needs scrutinizing and the experience of those with whom he works in the different context in the diocese has to be considered. The bishop, therefore, may establish a board which has the task of seeing that his policy is implemented consistently. It would also ascertain the resource which he would require from synod in order to carry out this policy. Each of the main differentiated ministries would be represented, so that the experience of those being offered opportunities and their requirements could be brought to bear on the way in which the bishop's policy is executed. At the same time, since the board is acting on behalf of the bishop, he may nominate a person, chosen for his or her expertise, to represent each type of ministry.

This simple two-tiered system – consultative group and monitoring board – might seem to exclude the synod. But if it is acknowledged that ministry is the bishop's responsibility, then the structure should also demonstrate that. He would, however, be wise to recognize that the synod controls finance, and that therefore a synodical voice in the monitoring body is desirable. This would also ensure that some members of synod could speak with knowledge when questions of ministry and training are raised in synod. The choice of which differentiated ministries might be represented on the board would depend on those which are working in the diocese. On this basis it would be possible to resist token membership and encourage the board to work. And the question of links with other churches or with other diocesan departments could easily be negotiated. Since the board has so defined a task, it is possible to adjust its membership without implying too many political overtones. The vital point at all times is that the bishop's responsibility for the development of ministry in his diocese is the foundation of this structure.

The Design of a Draft Programme

There is no *tabula rasa* upon which to draw new proposals for the development of ministry. This outline, therefore, tries to move from present realities to some new ideas. That process, however, should not be confused with an endorsement of the *status quo*. Change can be brought about, particularly when the prior question of the church's task has been examined. In the performance of that task the various ministries have their differentiated roles. Five such are commonly found today: clergy, deaconesses and accredited lay ministers, laity, readers, and experimental ministries of various types. The order in which they are treated is not significant, for although the differentiation of ministries is important, this does not imply notions of hierarchy.

This section is about opportunities for learning and training. But behind this lies the assumption that questions of deployment and appointment are integral to the development of ministry. Training only has any sense within such a total context. Some may feel that the approach is too task oriented. But a task dominated stance does not preclude concern for the person. It does, however, provide a means by which sentience can be affirmed and used in the service of the task. If this issue is confused, the prevailing dependence will ensure that the training enterprise will shift into caring. Its capacity to absorb all available energies in this way is not something merely to be watched; one function of organization is to prevent this happening. In this complicated area where issues of training and of pastoral care meet, the model of ministry performs a unitive function. For if training is being offered and consistent exploration of ministry is being pursued, suitable provision will also be made for the support of these ministers. This is not a casual job. It is something for which deliberate provision has to be made in relation both to the demands of ministry and of the stresses of learning. At times of transition special concern for sentience is required. An example which may become increasingly important, is that of the shift in the ministry of women from that of a minority group seeking to offer something distinctive to the church to one of full participation in the systems of authorized ministry.

One further background point is that in each diocese there are other groups which think of themselves as doing training. These range from the social care department to the diocesan liturgical commission, apart from such voluntary associations as the Royal School of Church Music. Again, however, if there is a clear grasp of task such bodies may be seen as potential resource for the bishop's programme rather than as in competition with one another for clientele.

Five differentiated ministries were suggested. Although

for many purposes members from these ministries might be brought together for joint explorations of ministry, a reasoned perception of the task of each group and the grounds on which, when appropriate, they are combined, will contribute to a purposeful programme. This favourably contrasts with an apparently random series of events.

(a) Clergy

Out of the earlier discussion of the role of the clergy three areas of development become clear. First there is the acquisition of skills in leadership. Clergy need to reflect on how to engage with people and their expectations in order to lead them through the gospel to that mature dependence which is the mark of human obedience to God's will. Experiential group study of leadership and authority has a part to play in this. But it has to be acknowledged that even when this type of training was more acceptable in the church than it now is, it was not possible to involve all or even most of the clergy. This raises in an acute fashion the issue of how occasions for learning can be provided for those who, on the grounds of faith or on unconscious grounds of self-defence, resist the suggestion that the Christian leader needs to examine and be objective about the style of his leadership. Although direct involvement in experiential learning remains most desirable, it is also possible to incorporate into a programme, which includes a clear policy about the importance of leadership, a stance which may come to be recognized and shared by those taking part in other events. Participants in these will not directly be studying authority, leadership and organization, but through the way the courses and consultations are designed, managed and directed, they can become at least aware that such things matter. These issues are assigned such priority in a programme because ministers who stand by various defences, whether consciously or not, are less likely to be able to penetrate to members of contemporary society who have erected defences of their own against religion.

A second area of study is contemporary society. Any minister will need to appreciate his environment not in an abstract fashion but as it impinges on him. Sociological insights are useful here, but they are no substitute for skills in self-evaluation. To acquire techniques, however, will not be very productive unless the minister has made the model of ministry his own. Anyone who grasps what this is about will be motivated to learn and take part in evaluation. This is a difficult but important area. For self-evaluation is a stance and as such it is something almost inadvertently picked up from the prevailing ethos of ministry in a diocese. Skills are then learned not as additional techniques but as a result of a consistent experience of asking what is happening and why. Small, self-organized and motivated groups are probably the best way of sharing in such learning.

Thirdly there is theology. This is apparently the most traditional of skills and it may be that for clergy this will prove the way into the study of other aspects of their ministry and its development. Theological reflection is a permanent component of work on leadership and on understanding the environment in which that leadership is exercised. The parish clergy, however, also need to be informed about thinking in the various fields of theology. One way to do this is by means of a familiar style of learning – the lecture with questions. From such basic opportunities other chances for learning can arise. The bishop may also easily and publicly participate with his clergy in that partnership of learning. For if he attends the lectures, the significance of this fundamental discipline of theological study will be endorsed.

A number of practical consequences for programme design follow. There is no difference in approach between the training of junior clergy and others. This programme implies that all clergy, whatever their seniority, share a common vocation and a common responsibility for ministerial development. A useful distinction here is that between apprentice and authorized practitioner. An ordinand is an apprentice; but the moment he or she is publicly authorized, however limited their knowledge or skill, they are treated by people as practitioners. Nevertheless there is a sense in which these people are in a transitional phase of development in ministry. A programme which continues the pattern of college training, with lectures, reading and writing, does not take enough note of this. Hence a deliberate pushing of the neophyte to examine, both with his incumbent and from time to time with his peers and a consultant, what is happening to him in his new role and why, is more appropriate. Through such reflection the newly ordained can bring to bear their biblical, dogmatic and pastoral theology, which they have recently acquired at college, upon their experience of ministry. A pattern is thus set up for future study. This can be confirmed by a structure which introduces this stance to them as deacons, shifts responsibility for it to them in the second year, and in the third year incorporates them fully into the diocesan scheme.

Secondly, study by clergy need not necessarily be done away from the localities in which ministry is exercised. For some purposes a group meeting at a diocesan centre is appropriate. Courses offered by national and other bodies are sometimes valuable and clergy may be sponsored to them. But the locality is where issues of ministry arise and the stance that learning is integral to the practice of ministry is publicly affirmed when clergy train in their own localities. The guilt, too, which is felt (however misguidedly) by many ministers on leaving their parishes, even for a short while, can be minimized. It can then be made available for study as part of the evidence about the way ministry is being conceived. Chapters and similar groups, such as clergy societies, may create a sense of common endeavour and thus be used as points for learning. It is, however, questionable whether deanery chapters are suitable for this. They tend to be cluttered with issues as the House of Clergy and bring in various inter-parish rivalries. Self-selecting groups of local clergy may be a better basic context for learning about ministry.

A third consequence is that the bishop should work with invited groups of his clergy from time to time on the issues of the boundary between the church and society and the church's task. In this way he would be able to give substance to the shared responsibility for ministry. Such events would also begin to harness the feelings in the relationship between bishop and priest to the task of ministry, and thus give the whole idea of the development of ministry, rather

106

than merely of training, a public significance which it would otherwise be difficult to engender.

(b) Deaconesses and Accredited Lay Ministers

Any comment may only be diffidently risked on the development of the ministry of deaconesses and accredited lay ministers (who are usually female). The ordination of women looms so large that it seems almost to obliterate serious reflection on these roles in the church. Such people at present support and assist clergy; there is scarcely any other option open to them. But in so far as this assistance is offered in the parochial and sector ministries, virtually all the training offered to clergy will also be appropriate for them. There is, however, one distinctive question which relates less to their being female than to their being virtually permanent assistants. A clear parallel may be drawn between them and curates in the need to examine what it means to be an assistant in the context of high expectations of the right of access to the vicar or other leader. However these ministries may change in the future, that particular issue will remain for any assistant, whether male or female. This is an important area for study and learning, since leadership implies followership and the relationship between colleagues in a dependent environment is always subject to exploitation. So long, however, as these questions are obscured in the church by being seen in terms of male and female in ministry, serious investigation is going to be difficult. An example of the practical effect of this may be often seen in mixed groups of newly ordained ministers. As the men gain more confidence in ministry, they begin to think about ordination as priests and greater responsibilities in a new relationship with their incumbent as fellow priest. Accredited lay ministers and deaconesses, however, become increasingly aware of their limited role as assistants. There is a different training task for each group. Demands may be made that they stay together to share the pain of differences, but this is not training; such a group would require another justification.

(c) Laity

In lay development the two focuses of concern have already

been indicated: the life of the parish and communication with particular groups within society. A diocesan programme cannot let either of these go at the expense of the other. Much, therefore, seems to depend on how models of training can integrate these issues. One goal, therefore, will be to approach the question of lay training tangentially by providing the clergy with a model for training which they can employ in their local work with lay people. This constitutes that collaborative ministry which is so often admired, although this may not always be realized when some programmes are set up. For example, some dioceses offer general lay courses in theology which lead to a diocesan or bishop's certificate. This has little intrinsic value as a qualification and may encourage the belief that acquiring knowledge is a way to more effective ministry. Knowledge is not to be despised, but ministry is about using what one has rather than acquiring it for its own sake. One danger of such certificates is that qualifications are confused with authorization to minister. But collaborative ministry occurs when Christian people in their different roles work together by employing, not blurring, those differences. One such differentiation lies in the authority assigned rather than any qualification gained. A priest is not such because he has learned more or different things than a layman.

An example of how this distinction may be kept clear and one form of lay ministry stimulated comes from the way lay pastoral or liturgical assistants may be appointed. In some places there has been a request for the bishop to authorize such ministers. There is, however, a danger that for the highest motives the bishop's authority may be interposed between that of the priest and people and thus the fundamental working relationships of the church – bishop and priest, priest and people – might be subverted. Any plan, therefore, needs to conform more closely to an application of the model of ministry. The bishop would, therefore, determine a policy for lay ministries in his diocese and delegate to the clergy authority within that policy to authorize ministries within the parishes. Responsibility for any training would remain with the parish priest, who would, like the bishop, delegate aspects of this training role and utilize any suitable resource. This is a small instance of how by carefully considering the questions of authority which are raised by a desired development in ministry, it is possible to set up a genuinely collaborative system to achieve what is wished for without increasing problems. This is only possible if all concerned, and especially here the bishop and clergy, have grasped through their own learning the significance of the model and can therefore also make it the basis for their work at developing the local ministry of lay people. It is not just a matter of deciding on a new idea about lay ministry; it is crucial both for effective ministry and for lay learning that the intention and the task are felt to cohere.

Lay ministry, however, is also about being a Christian in the world. In general, training for this is not possible. The learning for survival occurs through worship, which forms the Christian character. Learning for development and for change comes about through living the Christian life, regardless of how competently or not, on others' terms. What, therefore, is required is a means by which lay people can bring their experiences back to the church and learn from them together what they and what God are doing. One way is consciously to recognize that in so doing they are not so much learning as teaching. For they educate one another and the clergy. This is a further example of genuinely collaborative ministry, in which differentiated roles are not in competition but are mobilized for the church's work. An extreme, but illuminating, example of how this might occur was in the experiment in theological education during the 1970s in Washington, DC. Laity in congregations were given clear roles in training ordinands and this was given organizational expression. It appears that ordinands were trained, but also that the lay people themselves, through doing this work, were themselves invigorated in their Christian lives outside the church.[1]

The function of a diocesan programme for lay training, therefore, is to hold an environment in which these two main thrusts can be nurtured. It can provide some resources, especially personnel and ideas, and can also stimulate thought and action. But since the bishop's authority, if it gets between priest and people, does not forward ministry, there is no place for a diocesan officer or programme to slip insidiously in there either. The recovery of confidence at this point is crucial for the church's work in all its aspects, and the primary task of any diocesan programme must be to ensure that this is possible.

(d) Readers

One authorized lay ministry is that of reader. In spite of one or two attempts to expand this ministry, it seems to become a repository for anxieties about the ordering of ministry in general. The discussions on whether readers should be deacons or lay, about their relationship with the non-stipendiary ministry, questions about their administering the sacraments – all seem to suggest that this ministry is used as a sump into which unresolved questions may be poured. Taking services is not necessarily an intellectually demanding occupation. There is no reason why anyone duly authorized should not lead non-eucharistic worship. This, therefore, is not a distinctive function of the reader. However, since the title and the exercise of this ministry, especially in preaching, imply some learning, and the training can be demanding, it would seem that this order may best be thought of as providing potentially some theological resource in the localities. If the role is defined first as such, with teaching and preaching as consequences, then the requirements for selection, training and continuing education become clear.

(e) Experimental Ministries

Experiments in ministry are notoriously problematical because they customarily raise issues on the boundary between the diocese (what the bishop believes needs to be done) and the wider church. The only experiment that has been nationally attempted is the non-stipendiary ministry. This exposes some of the issues. Although, for example, in principle the responsibility for the pre-ordination training of candidates is clear, in practice it can remain obscure. A diocese, may find itself providing teaching and pastoral support for its candidates on a local course, even though this is formally the course's responsibility. The fundamental issue is that of the distinctive task of such experimental ministries. Until this is clarified in each case, training will appear, and often be, haphazard. Now that there is a number of men and women in the non-stipendiary ministry it is becoming apparent that under the generic heading of NSM there is little, if any, common task or experience. It may be wise, therefore, to focus learning upon the experimental nature of such ministry. This may then be used as a yardstick both for the individual's ministry and for looking at the significance of the experiment for the ministry of the church as a whole. Learning may then be focused on the way in which such new ministries interact with others. In the case of the NSM, this might be on how the incumbent and his NSM relate in work, which is another instance of leadership, followership and mutual perceptions of the immediate task. Developments in new or experimental ministries will not be found in some theology of ministry which might be deduced from one or several sources. The clearer the church's awareness of the nature of its interaction with society becomes, the better it will be able to reflect upon the requirements of ministry, the importance of it as a symbol, and to develop new approaches for testing.

NOTES

1   Celia Allison Hahn, ed., *Intermet: A Bold Experiment in Theological Education* (Washington DC, Intermet, 1977).

Conclusion

It would be possible at this point to conclude with a paragraph or two of apocalyptic vision, whether of hope or despair, for the church and even for the world. Such easy generalizations, however, are at complete variance with the intention of this book. Throughout attention has been focused on what really is the case, on evidence and its interpretation, and upon ways of organizing for work as a result of new understandings. The argument stands or falls as a whole: from task to organization, from institution to role, from vocation to the development of ministry. These are all interconnected.

The model of ministry leads away from exhortation to interpretation. When assumptions are consistently questioned and anxieties freely experienced against a coherent framework for this interpretation, then immediate change in response and attitude can come about in every instance of ministry and long-term structural development can also be embarked upon with confidence.

This stance not only needs to be grasped if the church is to minister effectively. It has also to be held as a matter of Christian commitment. For it is the model of ministry of Christ himself.

Further Reading

ON THE THEORY

Lawrence, W. G. ed., *Exploring Individual and Organisational Boundaries*. London and New York, John Wiley & Sons, 1979.

Miller, E. J. ed., *Task and Organisation*. London and New York, John Wiley & Sons, 1976.

Miller, E. J., and Rice, A. K., *Systems of Organisation*. London, Tavistock Publications, 1972.

Rice, A. K., *The Enterprise and its Environment*. London, Tavistock Publications, 1963.

ON THE CHURCH AND TRAINING

Gosling, R., Miller, D., Turquet, P. M., Woodhouse, D. L., *The Use of Small Groups in Training*. Hertford, Codicote Press, 1967.

Reed, B. D., *The Dynamics of Religion*. London, Darton, Longman & Todd, 1978.

Index